THE NEW YORK POETS

Frank O'Hara, John Ashbery, Kenneth Koch, James Schuyler

An Anthology

MARK FORD was born in 1962. His publications include two collections of poetry, *Landlocked* (Chatto & Windus, 1992, 1998), and *Soft Sift* (Faber & Faber, 2001/Harcourt Brace, 2003); a critical biography of the French poet, playwright and novelist Raymond Roussel (*Raymond Roussel and the Republic of Dreams*, Faber & Faber, 2000/Cornell University Press, 2001); a 20,000 word interview with John Ashbery (Between the Lines, 2003) and, for Carcanet, *'Why I am Not a Painter' and other poems*, a selection of the poetry of Frank O'Hara. Mark Ford is a regular contributor to the *Times Literary Supplement* and the *London Review of Books*. He teaches in the English department at University College London.

THE NEW YORK POETS

Frank O'Hara, John Ashbery,
Kenneth Koch, James Schuyler
An Anthology

Edited with an introduction by
MARK FORD

CARCANET

This selection first published in Great Britain in 2004 by
Carcanet Press Limited
Alliance House
Cross Street
Manchester M2 7AQ

A CIP catalogue record for this book is available from the British Library

ISBN 1 85754 734 9

The publisher acknowledges financial assistance from Arts Council England

Typeset by XL Publishing Services, Tiverton
Printed and bound in England by SRP Ltd, Exeter

CONTENTS

Frank O'Hara

John Ashbery

Kenneth Koch

James Schuyler

INTRODUCTION

The term 'The New York School of Poets' was first used in 1961, in an article by John Bernard Myers published in the Californian magazine *Nomad*. Myers was a hugely energetic impresario of the avant-garde: in the 1940s he'd both edited a poetry magazine called *Upstate,* and been managing editor of the Surrealist *View,* set up by Charles Henri Ford and Parker Tyler under the aegis of André Breton. In 1950 he co-founded the Tibor de Nagy Gallery in Manhattan. On the advice of the likes of Clement Greenberg and Willem de Kooning, he assembled an impressive stable of painters that included Fairfield Porter, Larry Rivers, Helen Frankenthaler, and Grace Hartigan. Around the same time Myers also launched a four-page poetry broadside, *Semi-Colon,* and began issuing limited editions of chapbooks that combined the work of a poet and painter. Among the first of these were Frank O'Hara's *A City Winter* (1952) illustrated by Larry Rivers, Kenneth Koch's *Poems* (1953) with prints by Nell Blaine, and John Ashbery's *Turandot and Other Poems* (1953), which included four drawings by Jane Freilicher.

'The New York School of Painters' was a label loosely used to denote the work of abstract expressionists such as Jackson Pollock, Willem de Kooning, Barnett Newman, Mark Rothko, Robert Motherwell, and Franz Kline. Part joke, part provocative assertion of New World supremacy over the School of Paris, it proved immensely effective in promoting the innovations of post-war New York artists to both national and international audiences. Myers no doubt reasoned a similar tactic might help raise the profile of these hitherto neglected experimental poets, who were all interested in avant-garde painting – indeed involved, to varying degrees, in the professional art world: Frank O'Hara worked for over a decade at the Museum of Modern Art, where he was eventually made an Associate Curator, and he frequently collaborated with painters such as Mike Goldberg, Joe Brainard and Larry Rivers; Kenneth Koch also participated in numerous art and theatrical collaborations, and in his late autobiographical poem, 'A Time Zone', talks with particular frankness about the inspiration he derived from the New York art scene of the 1950s; John Ashbery earned his keep for most of his life as an art critic for, among others, the international edition of

The New York Herald Tribune, Art News (where he was also executive editor from 1965 to 1972), and *Newsweek*; and the only reasonably regular jobs ever held by James Schuyler were at the Museum of Modern Art, where he worked on the front desk and in the International Program, and as a reviewer for *Art News*, for which he wrote several hundred pieces between 1955 and 1978. 'New York poets,' Schuyler commented in 1959, 'except I suppose the color blind, are affected most by the floods of paint in whose crashing surf we all scramble.'

'The New York School of Poets' is both a useful label, and something of a misnomer. Whereas most avant-garde literary movements of the twentieth century codified their aims in manifestos explaining their political and aesthetic principles, Ashbery, O'Hara, Koch, and Schuyler studiously avoided serious theorising or earnest justifications of their poetic practices. 'We were', as Ashbery put it in his *Paris Review* interview of 1983, 'a bunch of poets who happened to know each other; we would get together and read our poems to each other and sometimes we would write collaborations.' Unlike the Surrealists or the Language Movement poets, they never set out in any programmatic way to revolutionise society or consciousness: the only programme their work might be said to fulfil is the resolute determination to be unprogrammatic. 'You just go on your nerve,' as O'Hara explained in his hilarious mock-manifesto, 'Personism': 'If someone's chasing you down the street with a knife you just run, you don't turn around and shout, "Give it up! I was a track star for Mineola Prep!"'

And if the implications of 'school' are comically inappropriate when applied to the work of poets who, in the main, ignored or derided academia and the temptations of poetic high seriousness, the suggestion that their work is exclusively concerned with New York is also misleading. Frank O'Hara, it is true, wrote obsessively about Manhattan, and as fully deserves to be called the poet of mid-twentieth-century New York as Baudelaire does the poet of mid-nineteenth-century Paris. He cultivated numerous passionate friendships with a diverse circle of New York-based artist-friends – dancers, painters, musicians, poets – who formed a kind of coterie his poetry both celebrates and helps to keep creatively 'humming'. O'Hara, like his great hero Apollinaire, loved acting as a catalyst to an extended artistic circle, and poems such as 'Why I Am Not a Painter' and 'Radio' in turn pay poetic tribute to the powers of his *confrères* to inspire him. At times the city itself is addressed as a somewhat temperamental artist or lover:

How funny you are today New York
like Ginger Rogers in *Swingtime*
and St. Bridget's steeple leaning a little to the left...

Eventually it returned the compliment: 'One need never leave the confines of New York', O'Hara wrote in the prose poem 'Meditations in an Emergency', 'to get all the greenery one wishes – I can't even enjoy a blade of grass unless I know there's a subway handy, or a record store or some other sign that people do not totally *regret* life.' This sentence was engraved on a commemorative plaque in Lower Manhattan's Battery Park some two decades after O'Hara's death in a freak beach-buggy accident on Fire Island in the summer of 1966.

O'Hara constantly makes us aware of the importance of New York to his poetry and identity, and Koch also, in poems of reminiscence such as 'Fate', 'To Marina' and 'The Circus', creates a sense of New York in the 1950s as a uniquely creative and formative ferment of ideas and people: 'it was the Renaissance,' he boldly declares towards the end of 'To Marina'. His more surrealistic long poems, however, such as 'A New Guide' or his book-length mock-epics *Ko, or A Season on Earth* (1959) or *The Duplications* (1977) unfurl in a free-floating country of the mind far removed from the imperatives of New York life. And the more meditative Ashbery and Schuyler rarely attempt O'Hara's full-frontal identification with the city. Ashbery spent most of the decade from 1955 to 1965 in Paris, and since 1979 has divided his time between Hudson, NY, and Manhattan. In 'Self-Portrait in a Convex Mirror' he describes New York as 'a logarithm of other cities', as both 'alive with filiations, shuttlings' and as the 'gibbous / Mirrored eye of an insect.' The paradoxes and confusions of New York make it for Ashbery a kind of 'anti-place, an abstract climate': 'once one was there, one didn't have to think about where one was', he remarked in an interview of 1977. In other words, for Ashbery it is the neutrality of New York that licenses his imagination to rove at will through the literal and cultural geography of America, from Cottage Grove, wherever that is ('Out here on Cottage Grove, it matters', begins 'Pyrography') to Adcock Corner and Story Book Farm ('The One Thing That Can Save America') to where 'Pistachio Avenue rams the 2300 block of Highland / Fling Terrace' in the seething, sublime jumble of places and names in 'Daffy Duck in Hollywood'.

Schuyler, the most literal and descriptive of the group, tends to view the city through the prisms of time and loss. 'When they tore down / the Singer Building', he laments in 'Dining Out with Doug and Frank',

and when I saw the Bogardus Building
rusty and coming unstitched in
a battlefield of rubble I deliberately

withdrew my emotional investments
in loving old New York.

'Except,' he adds, 'you can't.' Schuyler wrote many wonderfully delicate, often painfully enervated descriptions of Manhattan scenes and incidents, but the majority of his lyrics set about recording the shifting weather and landscape of his pastoral refuges in Long Island and Maine, while his three longest poems are set in Washington DC ('Hymn to Life') and in upstate New York ('The Morning of the Poem' and 'A Few Days').

New York City was, however, crucial to the evolution of their friendships and the place in which most of the poems in this book were written. None were native New Yorkers: Ashbery grew up on a farm near Sodus, in western New York State, Koch in Cincinnati, O'Hara in Grafton, Massachusetts, and Schuyler in Washington DC and East Aurora, a small town near Buffalo. Ashbery and Koch first met in 1947 at Harvard, where both were on the board of the *Advocate*. O'Hara also attended Harvard, on the GI Bill after a two-year stint in the US navy, but only met Ashbery shortly before the latter moved to New York (where Koch had already settled) on graduating in 1949. Schuyler, the oldest of the four, had also been in the navy, from which he went AWOL in 1944; at the hearing that followed his homosexuality was revealed, which led to his being discharged as 'undesirable'. He spent the years between 1947 and 1949 in Europe, mainly in Italy, where he worked for several months as W.H. Auden's secretary. Two years after his return to New York, at a party after the opening of Larry Rivers's first show at the Tibor de Nagy Gallery, he was introduced to both O'Hara and Ashbery, and the following year met Kenneth Koch. The four musketeers were complete.

Highly conscious that the kind of poetry they were writing ran radically counter to the New Critical orthodoxies of the day, they formed each other's only initial audiences. 'We inspired each other,' Koch later recalled, 'we envied each other, we emulated each other, we were very critical of each other, we admired each other, we were almost entirely dependent on each other for support. Each had to be better than the others, but if one flopped we all did.' They also took to collaborating: in 1952 Ashbery and Schuyler embarked on *A Nest of Ninnies*, a wittily sophisticated comedy of manners composed mainly in alternate sentences, which was eventually published in 1969; Ashbery and Koch wrote a number of poems together, including a sestina whose every line includes the name of a flower, a tree, a fruit, a game, a famous old lady, a reference to a piece of office furniture and the word *bathtub*. (This poem, 'Crone Rhapsody', appeared in a special issue devoted to collaborations of the magazine, *Locus Solus*, edited by Ashbery, Koch, Schuyler and the novelist Harry Mathews, which ran for five issues in the early 1960s.) Koch and O'Hara particularly relished poetic jousts, and composed their first long poems (*When the Sun Tries to Go On* and 'Second Avenue') in a kind of competitive dialogue, each goading the other to fresh flights of fancy. For both, poetry could happen any time, any place:

> A little hard-as-a-hat poem to the day we offer
> 'Sky / woof woof! / harp'
> This is repeated ten times
> Each word is one line so the whole poem is thirty lines
> It's a poem composed in a moment
> On the sidewalk about fifteen blocks from the Alice in Wonderland
> > Monument...
>
> 'A Time Zone'

The irreverence of the New York School writers is one of their most appealing qualities. In their reaction against the serious, ironic, ostentatiously well made lyric that dominated the post-war poetry scene, they turned to the work of an eclectic range of literary iconoclasts, eccentrics and experimenters. Had the woman who, after reading an article on their work in the *New York Times*, wrote to Kenneth Koch asking how to enrol in the New York School's poetry programme, been sent back a registration form and a reading list, the latter might have included the works of Antonin Artaud, Djuna Barnes, Thomas Lovell Beddoes, E.F. Benson, Mary Butts, John Cage, René Char, John Clare, Ronald Firbank, Jean Garrigue, Paul Goodman, Henry Green, Alfred Jarry, Max Jacob, V.R. Lang, Lautréamont, the invented Australian poet Ern Malley, Vladimir Mayakovsky, Pierre Reverdy, Marcelin Pleynet, F.T. Prince, Laura Riding, Arthur Rimbaud, Raymond Roussel, David Schubert, Gertrude Stein, Thomas Traherne, John Wheelwright, John Wieners – as well as more mainstream figures such as Auden (but only his early work), Elizabeth Bishop, Wallace Stevens, William Carlos Williams, Kafka, Proust and Pasternak. The poets they especially scorned were those East Coast formalists who, in James Schuyler's words, 'wishfully descend tum-ti-tumming from Yeats out of Graves with a big kiss for Mother England'. Kenneth Koch's 'Fresh Air' of 1955 memorably captures their impatience with the academic conservatism of the 1950s poetic establishment:

Where are young poets in America, they are trembling in publishing houses
        and universities,
Above all they are trembling in universities, they are bathing the library
        steps with their spit,
They are gargling out innocuous (to whom?) poems about maple trees and
        their children,
Sometimes they brave a subject like the Villa d'Este or a lighthouse in
        Rhode Island,
Oh what worms they are! They wish to perfect their form…

Here on the railroad train, one more time, is the Strangler,
He is going to get that one there, who is on his way to a poetry reading.
Agh! Biff! A body falls to the moving floor.

The verbal equivalents of Koch's strangler were the techniques derived from
European Surrealism that all four employed, particularly in their early work, as
a means of sabotaging contemporary poetic conventions. 'Yippee!' O'Hara
exclaims in 'Blocks':

        she is shooting in the harbor! he is jumping
up to the maelstrom! she is leaning over the giant's
cart of tears which like a lava cone let fall to fly
from the cross-eyed tantrum-tousled ninth grader's
splayed fist is freezing on the cement!

Koch is as fond as O'Hara of this kind of imagistic exuberance, but Ashbery, even
at his most disruptive in his second volume, *The Tennis Court Oath* (1962), tends
towards a more enigmatic, subliminally charged poetics of displacement and
fragmentation:

They dream only of America
To be lost among the thirteen million pillars of grass:
"This honey is delicious
Though it burns the throat."

And hiding from darkness in barns
They can be grownups now

And the murderer's ash tray is more easily—
The lake a lilac cube.

While O'Hara's energetic syntax crams together disparate elements into an exhil-
arating synaesthetic 'maelstrom', the different kinds of idiom spliced together in
Ashbery's lines create a mirage-like sense of the elusiveness of reality. Both
poems might be used to illustrate, however, the ways in which *la grande permis-
sion* of the French Surrealists could be appropriated, ploughed under, and melded
with the diverse, impure poetry of America.

As much as for Romantics such as Keats, the long poem was for the New York
poets 'the Polar Star of Poetry'. In his introduction to O'Hara's *Collected Poems*
Ashbery describes O'Hara's evolution of 'big, airy structures unlike anything
previous in American poetry and indeed unlike poetry, more like the inspired
ramblings of a mind open to the point of distraction.' Certainly the long poems
of Ashbery, O'Hara, Koch and Schuyler offer an extraordinary blend of excess
and insouciance, of artifice and the aleatory, but in this, it might be argued, they
continue within the parameters established by American poetry's primary epic
of inclusion, Whitman's 'Song of Myself': as in Whitman, the profoundly felt and
the casually noticed, the bizarre, the erotic, the random, the tragic and the banal
jostle together to evoke a densely layered, composite sense of time passing, of the
individual, history, nature, and society continually colliding and breaking apart.
The long poems I have chosen for this volume – O'Hara's 'In Memory of My
Feelings', Ashbery's 'Self-Portrait in a Convex Mirror', Koch's 'To Marina', and
Schuyler's 'Hymn to Life' – are among their shorter explorations of the genre, but
will, I hope, induce readers to seek out the likes of Ashbery's *Flow Chart*,
Schuyler's 'The Morning of the Poem', Koch's *The Duplications*, and O'Hara's last
long series of 'inspired ramblings', 'Biotherm (For Bill Berkson)'.

'Grace', O'Hara writes in 'In Memory of My Feelings', punning on the name
of his friend Grace Hartigan, 'to be born and live as variously as possible.' The
phrase is engraved on his headstone in Green River Cemetery on Long Island.
His shockingly painful death inspired one of Schuyler's finest poems, 'Buried at
Springs', an elegy which slides effortlessly from an evocative description of the
day to a powerfully restrained articulation of suffering and loss:

a day like a gull passing
with a slow flapping of wings
in a kind of lope, without

breeze enough to shake loose
the last of the fireweed flowers,
a faintly clammy day, like wet silk
stained by one dead branch
the harsh russet of dried blood.

O'Hara was forty when he died, and had published only a handful of slim volumes and chapbooks. He had, however, attracted an ardent band of followers – poets such as Ron Padgett, Ted Berrigan, Tony Towle and Frank Lima – who came to form what some have called the second generation of the New York School. It was not, though, until his massive *Collected Poems* appeared in 1971, and won the National Book Award, that the full scope and ambition of his work became clear. It was around the same time that John Ashbery found himself hailed by a range of critics, including Harold Bloom who boldly declared Ashbery the most genuine heir of Wallace Stevens, and the poet of his generation most likely 'to survive the severe judgments of time'. The 1970s canonisation of Ashbery and O'Hara has tended to obscure the importance of their relationships with Koch and Schuyler; one of the aims of this volume is to allow readers a sense of the way their poems fit together, echo and answer each other, make sly or camp jokes, go to the movies, the ballet, to vernissages or to the Hamptons together, or simply swap quotes from the day's papers: 'once under the pie plate tree,' Schuyler recalls in 'To Frank O'Hara',

it broke you up to read Sophie Tucker

—with the *Times* in a hammock—
had a gold tea service. "It's way out
on the nut," she said, "for service,
but it was my dream."

'*La poésie*', declared Lautréamont '*doit être faite par tous*' – a maxim used by the editors of *Locus Solus* as an epigraph to their issue devoted to collaborations. By the same token, anything can become material for a poem, from a newspaper billboard announcing the breakdown of a movie star ('Poem (Lana Turner has collapsed)') to a decision to make more toast ('June 30, 1974'), from a railroad crossing sign in Kenya ('One Train May Hide Another') to the latest antics of Popeye and Wimpy ('Farm Implements and Rutabagas in a Landscape'). If it is this fundamental premise that unites the very different kinds of poetry written by O'Hara, Ashbery, Koch, and Schuyler, and has made their work so influential on the development of American poetry in recent decades, it is also crucial to the means whereby the 'being of [their] sentences', to adapt a line from Ashbery's 'Soonest Mended', both emerged from and defined 'the climate that fostered them'.

Mark Ford

SELECT BIBLIOGRAPHY

Frank O'Hara

Poetry

A City Winter and Other Poems (New York: Tibor de Nagy Gallery Editions, 1951 [*sic*, i.e. 1952])

Oranges: 12 pastorals (New York: Tibor de Nagy Gallery Editions, 1953; New York: Angel Hair Books, 1969)

Meditations in an Emergency (New York: Grove Press, 1957; 1967)

Second Avenue (New York: Totem Press in Association with Corinth Books, 1960)

Odes (New York: Tiber Press, 1960)

Lunch Poems (San Francisco: City Lights Books, The Pocket Poets Series (No. 19), 1964)

Love Poems (Tentative Title) (New York: Tibor de Nagy Gallery Editions, 1965)

In Memory of My Feelings (New York: The Museum of Modern Art, 1967)

The Collected Poems of Frank O'Hara. Ed. Donald Allen (New York: Knopf, 1971; Berkeley: University of California Press, 1995)

The Selected Poems of Frank O'Hara. Ed. Donald Allen (New York: Knopf, 1974; Vintage Books, 1974; Manchester: Carcanet, 1991; London: Penguin Books, 1994)

Early Writing. Ed. Donald Allen (San Francisco: Grey Fox Press, 1977)

Poems Retrieved. Ed. Donald Allen (San Francisco: Grey Fox Press, 1977)

Selected Plays. Ed. Ron Padgett, Joan Simon, and Anne Waldman (1st ed. New York: Full Court Press, 1978) 2nd ed. titled *Amorous Nightmares of Delay: Selected Plays* (Baltimore, MD: Johns Hopkins University Press, 1997)

Hymns of St. Bridget. Co-written with Bill Berkson (Woodacre, CA: The Owl Press, 2001)

'Why I Am Not a Painter' and other poems. Ed. Mark Ford (Manchester: Carcanet, 2003)

Prose

Jackson Pollock (New York: George Braziller, Inc. 1959)

New Spanish painting and sculpture (New York: The Museum of Modern Art, 1960)

Nakian (New York: The Museum of Modern Art, 1966)
Art Chronicles, 1954–1966 (New York: G. Braziller, 1975)
Standing Still and Walking in New York. Ed. Donald Allen (San Franciso: Grey Fox Press, 1975)
What's With Modern Art? Selected Short Reviews & Other Art Writings. Ed. Bill Berkson (Austin, Texas: Mike and Dale's Press, 1999)

John Ashbery

Poetry

Turandot and Other Poems (New York: Tibor de Nagy Gallery Editions, 1953)
Some Trees (New Haven, CT: Yale University Press, 1956; New York: Corinth Books, 1970; New York: Ecco Press, 1978)
The Tennis Court Oath (Middleton, CT: Wesleyan University Press, 1962; New York: Columbia University Press, 1980; Lebanon, NH: University Press of New England, 1997)
Rivers and Mountains (New York: Holt, Rinehart and Winston, 1966; New York: Ecco Press, 1977, 1989)
The Double Dream of Spring (New York: E.P. Dutton & Co., 1970; New York: Ecco Press, 1976)
Three Poems (New York: Viking Press, 1972; Middlesex and New York: Penguin Books, 1977; New York: Ecco Press, 1989)
The Vermont Notebook. With Joe Brainard (Los Angeles: Black Sparrow Press, 1975; New York: Granary Books / Calais, VT: Z Press, 2001)
Self-Portrait in a Convex Mirror (New York: Viking Press, 1975; Manchester: Carcanet, 1977)
Houseboat Days (New York: Viking Press / Harmondsworth: Penguin Books, 1977; New York: Farrar, Straus and Giroux, 1999)
As We Know (New York: Viking Press, 1979; Manchester: Carcanet, 1981; New York; Farrar, Straus and Giroux, 1999)
Shadow Train (New York: Viking Press, 1981; Manchester: Carcanet, 1982)
A Wave (New York: Viking Press, 1984; Manchester: Carcanet, 1984; New York: Farrar, Straus and Giroux, 1998)
Selected Poems (New York: Viking Press; Manchester: Carcanet, 1986; London: Paladin, 1987 (expanded edition))
April Galleons (New York: Viking Press, 1987; Manchester: Carcanet, 1988; New York: Farrar, Straus and Giroux, 1998)
Flow Chart (New York: Knopf, 1991; Manchester: Carcanet, 1991; New York: Farrar, Straus and Giroux, 1998)

Hotel Lautréamont (New York: Knopf, 1992; Manchester: Carcanet, 1992; New York: Farrar, Straus and Giroux, 2000)

And The Stars Were Shining (New York: Farrar, Straus and Giroux, 1994; Manchester: Carcanet, 1994)

Can You Hear, Bird (New York: Farrar, Straus and Giroux, 1995; Manchester: Carcanet, 1995)

Wakefulness (New York: Farrar, Straus and Giroux, 1998; Manchester: Carcanet, 1998)

Girls on the Run (New York: Farrar, Straus and Giroux, 1999; Manchester: Carcanet, 1999)

Your Name Here (New York: Farrar, Straus and Giroux, 2000; Manchester: Carcanet, 2000)

Chinese Whispers (New York: Farrar, Straus and Giroux, 2002; Manchester: Carcanet, 2002)

Prose

A Nest of Ninnies. Co-written with James Schuyler (New York: Dutton, 1969; Manchester: Carcanet, 1987)

Three Plays (Calais, VT: Z Press, 1978; Manchester: Carcanet, 1988)

Reported Sightings, Art Chronicles 1957–1987. Ed. David Bergman (New York: Knopf, 1989; Manchester: Carcanet, 1989)

Other Traditions (Cambridge, MA: Harvard University Press, 2000)

Kenneth Koch

Poetry

Poems (New York: Tibor de Nagy Gallery Editions, 1953)

Ko: or, A Season on Earth (New York: Grove Press, 1959)

Thank You and Other Poems (New York: Grove Press, 1962)

When the Sun Tries to Go On (Santa Rosa: Black Sparrow Press, 1969)

The Pleasures of Peace and Other Poems (New York: Random House, 1969)

The Art of Love (New York: Random House, 1975)

The Duplications (New York: Random House, 1977)

The Burning Mystery of Anna in 1951 (New York: Random House, 1979)

Days and Nights (New York: Random House, 1982)

Selected Poems 1950–82 (New York: Vintage Books, 1985; Manchester: Carcanet, 1991)

On The Edge (New York: Viking Press, 1986)

Seasons on Earth (New York: Viking Press, 1987)

One Train (New York: Knopf, 1994; Manchester: Carcanet, 1997)
On the Great Atlantic Rainway: Selected Poems 1950–88 (New York: Knopf, 1994)
Straits (New York: Knopf, 1998)
New Addresses (New York: Knopf, 2000)
A Possible World (New York: Knopf, 2002)
Sun Out: Selected Poems, 1952–1954 (New York: Knopf, 2002)

Prose

Wishes, Lies and Dreams: Teaching Children to Write Poetry (New York: Random House, 1970)
Rose, Where Did You Get That Red?: Teaching Great Poetry to Children (New York: Random House, 1973)
I Never Told Anybody: Teaching Poetry Writing in a Nursing Home (New York: Random House, 1977)
Hotel Lambosa and Other Stories (New York: Coffee House Press, 1993)
The Art of Poetry: Poems, Parodies, Interviews, Essays and Other Work (Ann Arbor: University of Michigan Press, 1996)
Making Your Own Days: The Pleasures of Reading and Writing Poetry (New York: Simon and Schuster, 1999)

Drama

A Change of Hearts and Other Plays (New York: Vintage, 1973)
The Red Robins (New York: Random House, 1975)
One Thousand Avant-Garde Plays (New York: Knopf, 1988)
The Gold Standard (New York: Knopf, 1995)

James Schuyler

Poetry

Salute (New York: Tiber Press, 1960)
May 24th or So (New York: Tibor de Nagy Gallery Editions, 1966)
Freely Espousing (Garden City, NY: Paris Review Editions / Doubleday, 1969; New York: SUN, 1979)
The Crystal Lithium (New York: Random House, 1972)
Hymn to Life (New York: Random House, 1974)

The Home Book: Prose and Poems, 1951–1970. Ed. Trevor Winkfield (Calais, VT: Z Press, 1977)

The Morning of the Poem (New York: Farrar, Straus and Giroux, 1980)

A Few Days (New York: Random House, 1985)

Selected Poems (New York: Farrar, Straus and Giroux, 1988; Manchester: Carcanet, 1990)

Collected Poems (New York: Farrar, Straus and Giroux, 1993)

Prose

Alfred and Guinevere (New York: Harcourt, Brace, 1958; New York: New York Review of Books, 2002)

A Nest of Ninnies. Co-written with John Ashbery (New York: Dutton, 1969; Manchester: Carcanet, 1987)

What's For Dinner? (Santa Barbara, CA: Black Sparrow Press, 1978)

The Diary of James Schuyler. Ed. Nathan Kernan (Santa Rosa, CA: Black Sparrow Press, 1996)

Selected Art Writings. Ed. Simon Pettet (Santa Barbara, CA: Black Sparrow Press, 1998)

Secondary Reading

Berkson, Bill and Joe LeSueur, eds., *Homage to Frank O'Hara*. (Bolinas, CA: Big Sky, 1978)

Blasing, Mutlu Konuk, *Politics and Form in Postmodern Poetry: O'Hara, Bishop, Ashbery, and Merrill* (New York: Cambridge University Press, 1995)

Bloom, Harold, ed., *John Ashbery* (New York: Chelsea House, 1985)

Elledge, Jim, ed., *Frank O'Hara: To Be True To A City* (Ann Arbor: University of Michigan Press, 1990)

Feldman, Alan, *Frank O'Hara* (Boston: Twayne Publishers, 1979)

Ford, Mark, *John Ashbery in Conversation with Mark Ford* (London: Between the Lines, 2003)

Gooch, Brad, *City Poet: The Life and Times of Frank O'Hara* (New York: Knopf, 1993)

Herd, David, *John Ashbery and American Poetry* (Manchester: Manchester University Press, 2000)

Kermani, David, *John Ashbery: A Comprehensive Bibliography* (New York: Garland, 1976)

Lehman, David, *The Last Avant-Garde: The Making of the New York School of Poets* (New York: Doubleday, 1998)

Lehman, David, ed. *Beyond Amazement: New Essays on John Ashbery* (Ithaca: Cornell University Press, 1980)

LeSueur, Joe, *Digressions on Some Poems by Frank O'Hara* (New York: Farrar, Straus and Giroux, 2003)

Perloff, Marjorie, *Frank O'Hara: Poet Among Painters* (New York: G. Braziller, 1977; 1st paperback ed. Austin: University of Texas Press, 1979)

Schultz, Susan M., ed., *The Tribe of John: Ashbery and Contemporary Poetry* (Tuscaloosa: University of Alabama Press, 1995)

Shapiro, David, *John Ashbery: An Introduction to the Poetry* (New York: Columbia University Press, 1979)

Shoptaw, John, *On the Outside Looking Out: John Ashbery's Poetry* (Cambridge, MA: Harvard University Press, 1994)

Smith, Alexander, Jr., *Frank O'Hara: A Comprehensive Bibliography* (New York: Garland, 1979; 2nd printing, corrected, 1980)

Smith, Hazel, *Hyperscapes in the Poetry of Frank O'Hara: Difference, Homosexuality, Topography* (Liverpool: Liverpool University Press, 2000)

Ward, Geoff, *Statutes of Liberty: The New York School of Poets* (London: Macmillan; New York: St. Martin's Press, 1993)

Frank O'Hara

FRANK O'HARA

Frank O'Hara was born in Baltimore, Maryland in 1926, and grew up in Grafton, Massachusetts, where he attended the Catholic schools St Paul's and St John's High School. In 1944 he enlisted in the navy. O'Hara trained as a sonarman in Key West, and was deployed in the Pacific on the USS *Nicholas*. After the war he studied, on the GI Bill, at Harvard University, where he shared rooms with Edward Gorey. His first literary success occurred during his graduate studies at Ann Arbor: a manuscript entitled *A Byzantine Place* won the 1951 Avery Hopwood Major Award. O'Hara settled in New York that same year, and soon became the centre of a vibrant circle of poets, painters, musicians and dancers. Initially he worked at a variety of jobs – on the front desk at the Museum of Modern Art, as a secretary for Cecil Beaton, and as a reviewer for *Art News*. In 1955 he was offered a job as Administrative Assistant in MOMA's International Program, and over the next decade helped organise a number of travelling exhibitions, including, in 1958, the extremely influential 'The New American Painting' which featured the work of Willem de Kooning, Franz Kline, Jackson Pollock, Robert Motherwell, and Barnett Newman. His monograph on the work of Jackson Pollock was published in 1959, and his other writings on painting and sculpture are collected in *Art Chronicles 1954–1966* (1975) and in *Standing Still and Walking in New York* (1975). O'Hara's poems frequently refer to painters and painting, and the inspiration he derived from their work. In 'Why I Am Not a Painter' he contrasts the compositional processes of the abstract expressionist Mike Goldberg with his own approach to the writing of poetry.

O'Hara wrote an enormous amount, and normally at great speed. He was famous for being able to compose 'any time, any place', as James Schuyler once phrased it, even in the midst of conversations at parties. Only a fraction of his work appeared during his lifetime. His most popular volume was *Lunch Poems*, published by City Lights in 1964, which included a number of what he called his 'I do this, I do that' poems such as 'A Step Away From Them' and 'The Day Lady Died', a subtle and moving elegy for Billie Holiday. O'Hara also composed a number of poems, such as 'Homosexuality', explicitly about gay cruising, while

3

his lyric 'You Are Gorgeous and I'm Coming' is an acrostic on the name of his lover, the dancer Vincent Warren. O'Hara's poems are full of references to his artistic enthusiams, to the lives of his friends and lovers, to social events in Manhattan or the Hamptons, and to the latest productions of Hollywood. He was a passionate aficionado of the cinema: 'after all,' he commented in his spoof manifesto, 'Personism', 'only Whitman and Crane and Williams, of the American poets are better than the movies.' In poems such as 'To the Film Industry in Crisis' and 'Ave Maria' he pays extravagant homage to the 'glorious Silver Screen', and to favourite stars such as Mae West, Jeanette MacDonald, Elizabeth Taylor, and Jean Harlow. But beneath the bright, glamorous, seemingly casual surfaces of O'Hara's poems there often lurk all manner of unresolved conflicts, anxieties, and ambitions. In long poems such as 'In Memory of My Feelings' he overlays diverse figurations of the self to create an epic sense of both possibility and disorientation. His best work , as John Ashbery has suggested, is at once 'modest and monumental', a graceful, dramatic fusion of the performative and the spontaneous, of the poem's occasion and the poem itself.

O'Hara died after being struck by a jeep in the early hours of Sunday, 24 July 1966. The beach taxi in which his party was travelling after a night at a discotheque at Fire Island Pines broke down; as they waited for a replacement to arrive, O'Hara wandered off to look at the sea. A jeep approaching from the opposite direction swerved to avoid the stranded taxi and travellers, and hit O'Hara. He was taken by a police launch to Bayview General Hospital, where he died about forty hours later from his internal injuries. Among the mourners at his funeral in Green River Cemetery, East Hampton, were Robert Motherwell, Allen Ginsberg, Barnett Newman, Willem de Kooning, Adolf Gottlieb, Philip Guston, Alex Katz, Larry Rivers, John Ashbery and Kenneth Koch. His *Collected Poems*, edited by Donald Allen, was published in 1971, and won the National Book Award for Poetry.

Autobiographia Literaria

When I was a child
I played by myself in a
corner of the schoolyard
all alone.

I hated dolls and I
hated games, animals were
not friendly and birds
flew away.

If anyone was looking
for me I hid behind a
tree and cried out "I am
an orphan."

And here I am, the
center of all beauty!
writing these poems!
Imagine!

Poem

At night Chinamen jump
on Asia with a thump

while in our willful way
we, in secret, play

affectionate games and bruise
our knees like China's shoes.

The birds push apples through
grass the moon turns blue,

these apples roll beneath
our buttocks like a heath

full of Chinese thrushes
flushed from China's bushes.

As we love at night
birds sing out of sight,

Chinese rhythms beat
through us in our heat,

the apples and the birds
move us like soft words,

we couple in the grace
of that mysterious race.

Poem

The eager note on my door said "Call me,
call when you get in!" so I quickly threw
a few tangerines into my overnight bag,
straightened my eyelids and shoulders, and

headed straight for the door. It was autumn
by the time I got around the corner, oh all
unwilling to be either pertinent or bemused, but
the leaves were brighter than grass on the sidewalk!

Funny, I thought, that the lights are on this late
and the hall door open; still up at this hour, a
champion jai-alai player like himself? Oh fie!
for shame! What a host, so zealous! And he was

there in the hall, flat on a sheet of blood that
ran down the stairs. I did appreciate it. There are few
hosts who so thoroughly prepare to greet a guest
only casually invited, and that several months ago.

Memorial Day 1950

Picasso made me tough and quick, and the world;
just as in a minute plane trees are knocked down
outside my window by a crew of creators.
Once he got his axe going everyone was upset
enough to fight for the last ditch and heap
of rubbish.
           Through all that surgery I thought
I had a lot to say, and named several last things
Gertrude Stein hadn't had time for; but then
the war was over, those things had survived
and even when you're scared art is no dictionary.
Max Ernst told us that.
           How many trees and frying pans
I loved and lost! Guernica hollered look out!
but we were all busy hoping our eyes were talking
to Paul Klee. My mother and father asked me and
I told them from my tight blue pants we should
love only the stones, the sea, and heroic figures.
Wasted child! I'll club you on the shins! I
wasn't surprised when the older people entered
my cheap hotel room and broke my guitar and my can
of blue paint.
           At that time all of us began to think
with our bare hands and even with blood all over
them, we knew vertical from horizontal, we never
smeared anything except to find out how it lived.
Fathers of Dada! You carried shining erector sets
in your rough bony pockets, you were generous
and they were lovely as chewing gum or flowers!
Thank you!
           And those of us who thought poetry
was crap were throttled by Auden or Rimbaud
when, sent by some compulsive Juno, we tried
to play with collages or sprechstimme in their bed.
Poetry didn't tell me not to play with toys
but alone I could never have figured out that dolls
meant death.
           Our responsibilities did not begin
in dreams, though they began in bed. Love is first of all
a lesson in utility. I hear the sewage singing

underneath my bright white toilet seat and know
that somewhere sometime it will reach the sea:
gulls and swordfishes will find it richer than a river.
And airplanes are perfect mobiles, independent
of the breeze; crashing in flames they show us how
to be prodigal. O Boris Pasternak, it may be silly
to call to you, so tall in the Urals, but your voice
cleans our world, clearer to us than the hospital:
you sound above the factory's ambitious gargle.
Poetry is as useful as a machine!

                          Look at my room.
Guitar strings hold up pictures. I don't need
a piano to sing, and naming things is only the intention
to make things. A locomotive is more melodious
than a cello. I dress in oil cloth and read music
by Guillaume Apollinaire's clay candelabra. Now
my father is dead and has found out you must look things
in the belly, not in the eye. If only he had listened
to the men who made us, hollering like stuck pigs!

A Pleasant Thought from Whitehead

Here I am at my desk. The
light is bright enough
to read by it is a warm
friendly day I am feeling
assertive. I slip a few
poems into the pelican's
bill and he is off! out
the window into the blue!

The editor is delighted I
hear his clamor for more
but that is nothing. Ah!
reader! you open the page
my poems stare at you you
stare back, do you not? my
poems speak on the silver
of your eyes your eyes repeat
them to your lover's this
very night. Over your naked
shoulder the improving stars
read my poems and flash
then onward to a friend.

The eyes the poems of the
world are changed! Pelican!
you will read them too!

Blocks

1

Yippee! she is shooting in the harbor! he is jumping
up to the maelstrom! she is leaning over the giant's
cart of tears which like a lava cone let fall to fly
from the cross-eyed tantrum-tousled ninth grader's
splayed fist is freezing on the cement! he is throwing
up his arms in heavenly desperation, spacious Y of
his tumultuous love-nerves flailing like poinsettia in
its own nailish storm against the glass door of the
cumulus which is withholding her from these divine
pastures she has filled with the flesh of men as stones!
O fatal eagerness!

2

O boy, their childhood was like so many oatmeal cookies.
I need you, you need me, yum, yum. Anon it became suddenly

3

like someone always losing something and never knowing what.
Always so. They were so fond of eating bread and butter and
sugar, they were slobs, the mice used to lick the floorboards
after they went to bed, rolling their light tails against
the rattling marbles of granulation. Vivo! the dextrose
those children consumed, lavished, smoked, in their knobby
candy bars. Such pimples! such hardons! such moody loves.
And thus they grew like giggling fir trees.

Homosexuality

So we are taking off our masks, are we, and keeping
our mouths shut? as if we'd been pierced by a glance!

The song of an old cow is not more full of judgment
than the vapors which escape one's soul when one is sick;

so I pull the shadows around me like a puff
and crinkle my eyes as if at the most exquisite moment

of a very long opera, and then we are off!
without reproach and without hope that our delicate feet

will touch the earth again, let alone "very soon."
It is the law of my own voice I shall investigate.

I start like ice, my finger to my ear, my ear
to my heart, that proud cur at the garbage can

in the rain. It's wonderful to admire oneself
with complete candor, tallying up the merits of each

of the latrines. 14th Street is drunken and credulous,
53rd tries to tremble but is too at rest. The good

love a park and the inept a railway station,
and there are the divine ones who drag themselves up

and down the lengthening shadow of an Abyssinian head
in the dust, trailing their long elegant heels of hot air

crying to confuse the brave "It's a summer day,
and I want to be wanted more than anything else in the world."

Meditations in an Emergency

Am I to become profligate as if I were a blonde? Or religious as if I were French?

Each time my heart is broken it makes me feel more adventurous (and how the same names keep recurring on that interminable list!), but one of these days there'll be nothing left with which to venture forth.

Why should I share you? Why don't you get rid of someone else for a change?

I am the least difficult of men. All I want is boundless love.

Even trees understand me! Good heavens, I lie under them, too, don't I? I'm just like a pile of leaves.

However, I have never clogged myself with the praises of pastoral life, nor with nostalgia for an innocent past of perverted acts in pastures. No. One need never leave the confines of New York to get all the greenery one wishes—I can't even enjoy a blade of grass unless I know there's a subway handy, or a record store or some other sign that people do not totally *regret* life. It is more important to affirm the least sincere; the clouds get enough attention as it is and even they continue to pass. Do they know what they're missing? Uh huh.

My eyes are vague blue, like the sky, and change all the time; they are indiscriminate but fleeting, entirely specific and disloyal, so that no one trusts me. I am always looking away. Or again at something after it has given me up. It makes me restless and that makes me unhappy, but I cannot keep them still. If only I had gray, green, black, brown, yellow eyes; I would stay at home and do something. It's not that I'm curious. On the contrary, I am bored but it's my duty to be attentive, I am needed by things as the sky must be above the earth. And lately, so great has *their* anxiety become, I can spare myself little sleep.

Now there is only one man I love to kiss when he is unshaven. Heterosexuality! you are inexorably approaching. (How discourage her?)

St. Serapion, I wrap myself in the robes of your whiteness which is like midnight in Dostoevsky. How am I to become a legend, my dear? I've tried love, but that hides you in the bosom of another and I am always springing forth from it like the lotus—the ecstasy of always bursting forth! (but one must not be distracted by it!) or like a hyacinth, "to keep the filth of life away," yes, there, even in the heart, where the filth is pumped in and slanders and pollutes and determines. I will my will, though I may become famous for a mysterious vacancy in that department, that greenhouse.

Destroy yourself, if you don't know!

It is easy to be beautiful; it is difficult to appear so. I admire you, beloved, for the trap you've set. It's like a final chapter no one reads because the plot is over.

"Fanny Brown is run away—scampered off with a Cornet of Horse; I do love that little Minx, & hope She may be happy, tho' She has vexed me by this Exploit a little too.—Poor silly Cecchina! or F:B: as we used to call her.—I wish She had a good Whipping and 10,000 pounds."—Mrs. Thrale.

I've got to get out of here. I choose a piece of shawl and my dirtiest suntans. I'll be back, I'll re-emerge, defeated, from the valley; you don't want me to go where you go, so I go where you don't want me to. It's only afternoon, there's a lot ahead. There won't be any mail downstairs. Turning, I spit in the lock and the knob turns.

Music

If I rest for a moment near The Equestrian
pausing for a liver sausage sandwich in the Mayflower Shoppe,
that angel seems to be leading the horse into Bergdorf's
and I am naked as a table cloth, my nerves humming.
Close to the fear of war and the stars which have disappeared.
I have in my hands only 35¢, it's so meaningless to eat!
and gusts of water spray over the basins of leaves
like the hammers of a glass pianoforte. If I seem to you
to have lavender lips under the leaves of the world,
	I must tighten my belt.
It's like a locomotive on the march, the season
	of distress and clarity
and my door is open to the evenings of midwinter's
lightly falling snow over the newspapers.
Clasp me in your handkerchief like a tear, trumpet
of early afternoon! in the foggy autumn.
As they're putting up the Christmas trees on Park Avenue
I shall see my daydreams walking by with dogs in blankets,
put to some use before all those colored lights come on!
	But no more fountains and no more rain,
	and the stores stay open terribly late.

Poem

to James Schuyler

There I could never be a boy,
though I rode like a god when the horse reared.
At a cry from mother I fell to my knees!
there I fell, clumsy and sick and good,
though I bloomed on the back of a frightened black mare
who had leaped windily at the start of a leaf
and she never threw me.

I had a quick heart
and my thighs clutched her back.
I loved her fright, which was against me
into the air! and the diamond white of her forelock
which seemed to smart with thoughts as my heart smarted with life!
and she'd toss her head with the pain
and paw the air and champ the bit, as if I were Endymion
and she, moonlike, hated to love me.

All things are tragic
when a mother watches!
and she wishes upon herself
the random fears of a scarlet soul, as it breathes in and out
and nothing chokes, or breaks from triumph to triumph!

I knew her but I could not be a boy,
for in the billowing air I was fleet and green
riding blackly through the ethereal night
towards men's words which I gracefully understood,

and it was given to me
as the soul is given the hands
to hold the ribbons of life!
as miles streak by beneath the moon's sharp hooves
and I have mastered the speed and strength which is the armor of the world.

To the Harbormaster

I wanted to be sure to reach you;
though my ship was on the way it got caught
in some moorings. I am always tying up
and then deciding to depart. In storms and
at sunset, with the metallic coils of the tide
around my fathomless arms, I am unable
to understand the forms of my vanity
or I am hard alee with my Polish rudder
in my hand and the sun sinking. To
you I offer my hull and the tattered cordage
of my will. The terrible channels where
the wind drives me against the brown lips
of the reeds are not all behind me. Yet
I trust the sanity of my vessel; and
if it sinks, it may well be in answer
to the reasoning of the eternal voices,
the waves which have kept me from reaching you.

At the Old Place

Joe is restless and so am I, so restless.
Button's buddy lips frame "L G T TH O P?"
across the bar. "Yes!" I cry, for dancing's
my soul delight. (Feet! feet!) "Come on!"

Through the streets we skip like swallows.
Howard malingers. (Come on, Howard.) Ashes
malingers. (Come on, J.A.) Dick malingers.
(Come on, Dick.) Alvin darts ahead. (Wait up,
Alvin.) Jack, Earl and Someone don't come.

Down the dark stairs drifts the steaming cha-
cha-cha. Through the urine and smoke we charge
to the floor. Wrapped in Ashes' arms I glide.
(It's heaven!) Button lindys with me. (It's
heaven!) Joe's two-steps, too, are incredible,
and then a fast rhumba with Alvin, like skipping
on toothpicks. And the interminable intermissions,

we have them. Jack, Earl and Someone drift
guiltily in. "I knew they were gay
the minute I laid eyes on them!" screams John.
How ashamed they are of us!   we hope.

My Heart

I'm not going to cry all the time
nor shall I laugh all the time,
I don't prefer one "strain" to another.
I'd have the immediacy of a bad movie,
not just a sleeper, but also the big,
overproduced first-run kind. I want to be
at least as alive as the vulgar. And if
some aficionado of my mess says "That's
not like Frank!", all to the good! I
don't wear brown and gray suits all the time,
do I? No. I wear workshirts to the opera,
often. I want my feet to be bare,
I want my face to be shaven, and my heart—
you can't plan on the heart, but
the better part of it, my poetry, is open.

To the Film Industry in Crisis

Not you, lean quarterlies and swarthy periodicals
with your studious incursions toward the pomposity of ants,
nor you, experimental theatre in which Emotive Fruition
is wedding Poetic Insight perpetually, not you,
promenading Grand Opera, obvious as an ear (though you
are close to my heart), but you, Motion Picture Industry,
it's you I love!

In times of crisis, we must all decide again and again whom we love.
And give credit where it's due: not to my starched nurse, who taught me
how to be bad and not bad rather than good (and has lately availed
herself of this information), not to the Catholic Church
which is at best an oversolemn introduction to cosmic entertainment,
not to the American Legion, which hates everybody, but to you,
glorious Silver Screen, tragic Technicolor, amorous Cinemascope,
stretching Vistavision and startling Stereophonic Sound, with all
your heavenly dimensions and reverberations and iconoclasms! To
Richard Barthelmess as the "tol'able" boy barefoot and in pants,
Jeanette MacDonald of the flaming hair and lips and long, long neck,
Sue Carroll as she sits for eternity on the damaged fender of a car
and smiles, Ginger Rogers with her pageboy bob like a sausage
on her shuffling shoulders, peach-melba-voiced Fred Astaire of the feet,
Eric von Stroheim, the seducer of mountain-climbers' gasping spouses,
the Tarzans, each and every one of you (I cannot bring myself to prefer
Johnny Weissmuller to Lex Barker, I cannot!), Mae West in a furry sled,
her bordello radiance and bland remarks, Rudolph Valentino of the moon,
its crushing passions, and moonlike, too, the gentle Norma Shearer,
Miriam Hopkins dropping her champagne glass off Joel McCrea's yacht
and crying into the dappled sea, Clark Gable rescuing Gene Tierney
from Russia and Allan Jones rescuing Kitty Carlisle from Harpo Marx,
Cornel Wilde coughing blood on the piano keys while Merle Oberon berates,
Marilyn Monroe in her little spike heels reeling through Niagara Falls,
Joseph Cotten puzzling and Orson Welles puzzled and Dolores Del Rio
eating orchids for lunch and breaking mirrors, Gloria Swanson reclining,
and Jean Harlow reclining and wiggling, and Alice Faye reclining
and wiggling and singing, Myrna Loy being calm and wise, William Powell
in his stunning urbanity, Elizabeth Taylor blossoming, yes, to you

and to all you others, the great, the near-great, the featured, the extras
who pass quickly and return in dreams saying your one or two lines,

my love!
Long may you illumine space with your marvellous appearances, delays
and enunciations, and may the money of the world glitteringly cover you
as you rest after a long day under the kleig lights with your faces
in packs for our edification, the way the clouds come often at night
but the heavens operate on the star system. It is a divine precedent
you perpetuate! Roll on, reels of celluloid, as the great earth rolls on!

Radio

Why do you play such dreary music
on Saturday afternoon, when tired
mortally tired I long for a little
reminder of immortal energy?
                              All
week long while I trudge fatiguingly
from desk to desk in the museum
you spill your miracles of Grieg
and Honegger on shut-ins.
                              Am I not
shut in too, and after a week
of work don't I deserve Prokofieff?

Well, I have my beautiful de Kooning
to aspire to. I think it has an orange
bed in it, more than the ear can hold.

In Memory of My Feelings

to Grace Hartigan

1

My quietness has a man in it, he is transparent
and he carries me quietly, like a gondola, through the streets.
He has several likenesses, like stars and years, like numerals.

My quietness has a number of naked selves,
so many pistols I have borrowed to protect myselves
from creatures who too readily recognize my weapons
and have murder in their heart!
                                              though in winter
they are warm as roses, in the desert
taste of chilled anisette.
                                    At times, withdrawn,
I rise into the cool skies
and gaze on at the imponderable world with the simple identification
of my colleagues, the mountains. Manfred climbs to my nape,
speaks, but I do not hear him,
                                          I'm too blue.
An elephant takes up his trumpet,
money flutters from the windows of cries, silk stretching its mirror
across shoulder blades. A gun is "fired."
                                                        One of me rushes
to window #13 and one of me raises his whip and one of me
flutters up from the center of the track amidst the pink flamingoes,
and underneath their hooves as they round the last turn my lips
are scarred and brown, brushed by tails, masked in dirt's lust,
definition, open mouths gasping for the cries of the bettors for the lungs
of earth.
            So many of my transparencies could not resist the race!
Terror in earth, dried mushrooms, pink feathers, tickets,
a flaking moon drifting across the muddied teeth,
the imperceptible moan of covered breathing,
                                                              love of the serpent!
I am underneath its leaves as the hunter crackles and pants
and bursts, as the barrage balloon drifts behind a cloud
and animal death whips out its flashlight,
                                                        whistling

and slipping the glove off the trigger hand. The serpent's eyes
redden at sight of those thorny fingernails, he is so smooth!
                                        My transparent selves
flail about like vipers in a pail, writhing and hissing
without panic, with a certain justice of response
and presently the aquiline serpent comes to resemble the Medusa.

                                2

The dead hunting
and the alive, ahunted.
                        My father, my uncle,
my grand-uncle and the several aunts. My
grand-aunt dying for me, like a talisman, in the war,
before I had even gone to Borneo
her blood vessels rushed to the surface
and burst like rockets over the wrinkled
invasion of the Australians, her eyes aslant
like the invaded, but blue like mine.
An atmosphere of supreme lucidity,
                                humanism,
the mere existence of emphasis,
                                a rusted barge
painted orange against the sea
full of Marines reciting the Arabian ideas
which are a proof in themselves of seasickness
which is a proof in itself of being hunted.
A hit? *ergo* swim.
                        My 10   my 19,
my 9,   and the several years. My
12 years since they all died, philosophically speaking.
And now the coolness of a mind
like a shuttered suite in the Grand Hotel
where mail arrives for my incognito,
                                whose façade
has been slipping into the Grand Canal for centuries;
rockets splay over a *sposalizio*,
                                fleeing into night
from their Chinese memories, and it is a celebration,
the trying desperately to count them as they die.
But who will stay to be these numbers
when all the lights are dead?

The most arid stretch is often richest,
the hand lifting towards a fig tree from hunger
                                        digging
and there is water, clear, supple, or there
deep in the sand where death sleeps, a murmurous bubbling
proclaims the blackness that will ease and burn.
You preferred the Arabs? but they didn't stay to count
their inventions, racing into sands, converting themselves into
so many,
            embracing, at Ramadan, the tenderest effigies of
themselves with penises shorn by the hundreds, like a camel
ravishing a goat.
                And the mountainous-minded Greeks could speak
of time as a river and step across it into Persia, leaving the pain
at home to be converted into statuary. I adore the Roman copies.
And the stench of the camel's spit I swallow,
and the stench of the whole goat. For we have advanced, France,
together into a new land, like the Greeks, where one feels nostalgic
for mere ideas, where truth lies on its deathbed like an uncle
and one of me has a sentimental longing for number,
as has another for the ball gowns of the Directoire and yet
another for "Destiny, Paris, destiny!"
                            or "Only a king may kill a king."

How many selves are there in a war hero asleep in names? under
a blanket of platoon and fleet, orderly. For every seaman
with one eye closed in fear and twitching arm at a sigh for Lord Nelson,
he is all dead; and now a meek subaltern writhes in his bedclothes
with the fury of a thousand, violating an insane mistress
who has only herself to offer his multitudes.
                                Rising,
he wraps himself in the burnoose of memories against the heat of life
and over the sands he goes to take an algebraic position *in re*
a sun of fear shining not too bravely. He will ask himself to
vote on fear before he feels a tremor,
                            as runners arrive from the mountains
bearing snow, proof that the mind's obsolescence is still capable
of intimacy. His mistress will follow him across the desert
like a goat, towards a mirage which is something familiar about
one of his innumerable wrists,
                            and lying in an oasis one day,
playing catch with coconuts, they suddenly smell oil.

Beneath these lives
the ardent lover of history hides,
                              tongue out
leaving a globe of spit on a taut spear of grass
and leaves off rattling his tail a moment
to admire this flag.
                    I'm looking for my Shanghai Lil.
Five years ago, enamored of fire-escapes, I went to Chicago,
an eventful trip: the fountains! the Art Institute, the Y
for both sexes, absent Christianity.
                              At 7, before Jane
was up, the copper lake stirred against the sides
of a Norwegian freighter; on the deck a few dirty men,
tired of night, watched themselves in the water
as years before the German prisoners on the *Prinz Eugen*
dappled the Pacific with their sores, painted purple
by a Naval doctor.
                    Beards growing, and the constant anxiety
over looks. I'll shave before she wakes up. Sam Goldwyn
spent $2,000,000 on Anna Sten, but Grushenka left America.
One of me is standing in the waves, an ocean bather,
or I am naked with a plate of devils at my hip.
                                        Grace
to be born and live as variously as possible. The conception
of the masque barely suggests the sordid identifications.
I am a Hittite in love with a horse. I don't know what blood's
in me I feel like an African prince I am a girl walking downstairs
in a red pleated dress with heels I am a champion taking a fall
I am a jockey with a sprained ass-hole I am the light mist
                              in which a face appears
and it is another face of blonde I am a baboon eating a banana
I am a dictator looking at his wife I am a doctor eating a child
and the child's mother smiling I am a Chinaman climbing a mountain
I am a child smelling his father's underwear I am an Indian
sleeping on a scalp
                    and my pony is stamping in the birches,
and I've just caught sight of the *Niña*, the *Pinta* and the *Santa Maria*.
                    What land is this, so free?
                                        I watch
the sea at the back of my eyes, near the spot where I think
in solitude as pine trees groan and support the enormous winds,

they are humming *L'Oiseau de feu!*
                    They look like gods, these whitemen,
and they are bringing me the horse I fell in love with on the frieze.

                              5

And now it is the serpent's turn.
I am not quite you, but almost, the opposite of visionary.
You are coiled around the central figure,
                              the heart
that bubbles with red ghosts, since to move is to love
and the scrutiny of all things is syllogistic,
the startled eyes of the dikdik, the bush full of white flags
fleeing a hunter,
                    which is our democracy
                              but the prey
is always fragile and like something, as a seashell can be
a great Courbet, if it wishes. To bend the ear of the outer world.

                              When you turn your head
can you feel your heels, undulating? that's what it is
to be a serpent. I haven't told you of the most beautiful things
in my lives, and watching the ripple of their loss disappear
along the shore, underneath ferns,
                              face downward in the ferns
my body, the naked host to my many selves, shot
by a guerrilla warrior or dumped from a car into ferns
which are themselves *journalières.*
                    The hero, trying to unhitch his parachute,
stumbles over me. It is our last embrace.
                              And yet
I have forgotten my loves, and chiefly that one, the cancerous
statue which my body could no longer contain,
                              against my will
                              against my love
become art,
          I could not change it into history
and so remember it,
                and I have lost what is always and everywhere
present, the scene of my selves, the occasion of these ruses,
which I myself and singly must now kill
                    and save the serpent in their midst.

A Step Away from Them

It's my lunch hour, so I go
for a walk among the hum-colored
cabs. First, down the sidewalk
where laborers feed their dirty
glistening torsos sandwiches
and Coca-Cola, with yellow helmets
on. They protect them from falling
bricks, I guess. Then onto the
avenue where skirts are flipping
above heels and blow up over
grates. The sun is hot, but the
cabs stir up the air. I look
at bargains in wristwatches. There
are cats playing in sawdust.
                                        On
to Times Square, where the sign
blows smoke over my head, and higher
the waterfall pours lightly. A
Negro stands in a doorway with a
toothpick, languorously agitating.
A blonde chorus girl clicks: he
smiles and rubs his chin. Everything
suddenly honks: it is 12:40 of
a Thursday.
                        Neon in daylight is a
great pleasure, as Edwin Denby would
write, as are light bulbs in daylight.
I stop for a cheeseburger at JULIET'S
CORNER. Guilietta Masina, wife of
Federico Fellini, *è bell' attrice.*
And chocolate malted. A lady in
foxes on such a day puts her poodle
in a cab.
                        There are several Puerto
Ricans on the avenue today, which
makes it beautiful and warm. First
Bunny died, then John Latouche,
then Jackson Pollock. But is the
earth as full as life was full, of them?
And one has eaten and one walks,

universalization

THE NEW YORK POETS

past the magazines with nudes
and the posters for BULLFIGHT and
the Manhattan Storage Warehouse,
which they'll soon tear down. I
used to think they had the Armory
Show there.
      A glass of papaya juice
and back to work. My heart is in my
pocket, it is Poems by Pierre Reverdy.

Why I Am Not a Painter

I am not a painter, I am a poet.
Why? I think I would rather be
a painter, but I am not. Well,

for instance, Mike Goldberg
is starting a painting. I drop in.
"Sit down and have a drink" he
says. I drink; we drink. I look
up. "You have SARDINES in it."
"Yes, it needed something there."
"Oh." I go and the days go by
and I drop in again. The painting
is going on, and I go, and the days
go by. I drop in. The painting is
finished. "Where's SARDINES?"
All that's left is just
letters, "It was too much," Mike says.

But me? One day I am thinking of
a color: orange. I write a line
about orange. Pretty soon it is a
whole page of words, not lines.
Then another page. There should be
so much more, not of orange, of
words, of how terrible orange is
and life. Days go by. It is even in
prose, I am a real poet. My poem
is finished and I haven't mentioned
orange yet. It's twelve poems, I call it
ORANGES. And one day in a gallery
I see Mike's painting, called SARDINES.

Poem Read at Joan Mitchell's

At last you are tired of being single
the effort to be new does not upset you nor the effort to be other
you are not tired of life together

city noises are louder because you are together
being together you are louder than calling separately across a tele-
            phone one to the other
and there is no noise like the rare silence when you both sleep
even country noises—a dog bays at the moon, but when it loves the
            moon it bows, and the hitherto frowning moon fawns and slips

Only you in New York are not boring tonight
it is most modern to affirm some one
(we don't really love ideas, do we?)
and Joan was surprising you with a party for which I was the decoy
but you were surprising us by getting married and going away
so I am here reading poetry anyway
and no one will be bored tonight by me because you're here

Yesterday I felt very tired from being at the FIVE SPOT
and today I felt very tired from going to bed early and reading ULYSSES
but tonight I feel energetic because I'm sort of the bugle,
like waking people up, of your peculiar desire to get married

It's so
original, hydrogenic, anthropomorphic, fiscal, post-anti-esthetic,
            bland, unpicturesque and WilliamCarlosWilliamsian!
it's definitely not 19th Century, it's not even Partisan Review, it's
            new, it must be vanguard!

Tonight you probably walked over here from Bethune Street
down Greenwich Avenue with its sneaky little bars and the Women's De-
            tention House,
across 8th Street, by the acres of books and pillows and shoes and
            illuminating lampshades,
past Cooper Union where we heard the piece by Mortie Feldman with
            "The Stars and Stripes Forever" in it
and the Sagamore's terrific "coffee and, Andy," meaning "with a cheese
            Danish"—

did you spit on your index fingers and rub the CEDAR's neon circle for
        luck?
did you give a kind thought, hurrying, to Alger Hiss?

It's the day before February 17th
it is not snowing yet but it is dark and may snow yet
dreary February of the exhaustion from parties and the exceptional de-
                sire for spring which the ballet alone, by extending its run,
                has made bearable, dear New York City Ballet company, you are
                quite a bit like a wedding yourself!
and the only signs of spring are Maria Tallchief's rhinestones and a
                perky little dog barking in a bar, here and there eyes which
                suddenly light up with blue, like a ripple subsiding under a
                lily pad, or with brown, like a freshly plowed field we vow
                we'll drive out and look at when a certain Sunday comes in May—
and these eyes are undoubtedly Jane's and Joe's because they are ad-
                vancing into spring before us and tomorrow is Sunday

This poem goes on too long because our friendship has been long, long
                for this life and these times, long as art is long and un-
                interruptable,
and I would make it as long as I hope our friendship lasts if I could
                make poems that long

I hope there will be more
more drives to Bear Mountain and searches for hamburgers, more evenings
                avoiding the latest Japanese movie and watching Helen Vinson
                and Warner Baxter in *Vogues of 1938* instead, more discussions
                in lobbies of the respective greatnesses of Diana Adams and
                Allegra Kent,
more sunburns and more half-mile swims in which Joe beats me as Jane
                watches, lotion-covered and sleepy, more arguments over
                Faulkner's inferiority to Tolstoy while sand gets into my
                bathing trunks
let's advance and change everything, but leave these little oases in
                case the heart gets thirsty en route
and I should probably propose myself as a godfather if you have any
                children, since I will probably earn more money some day
                accidentally, and could teach him or her how to swim
and now there is a Glazunov symphony on the radio and I think of our
                friends who are not here, of John and the nuptial quality
                of his verses (he is always marrying the whole world) and
                Janice and Kenneth, smiling and laughing, respectively (they

are probably laughing at the Leaning Tower right now)
but we are all here and have their proxy
if Kenneth were writing this he would point out how art has changed
women and women have changed art and men, but men haven't
changed women much
but ideas are obscure and nothing should be obscure tonight
you will live half the year in a house by the sea and half the year in
a house in our arms
we peer into the future and see you happy and hope it is a sign that we
will be happy too, something to cling to, happiness
the least and best of human attainments

Anxiety

I'm having a real day of it.
                              There was
something I had to do. But what?
There are no alternatives, just
the one something.
                   I have a drink,
it doesn't help—far from it!
                              I
feel worse. I can't remember how
I felt, so perhaps I feel better.
No. Just a little darker.
                         If I could
get really dark, richly dark, like
being drunk, that's the best that's
open as a field. Not the best,

but the best except for the impossible
pure light, to be as if above a vast
prairie, rushing and pausing over
the tiny golden heads in deep grass.

But still now, familiar laughter low
from a dark face, affection human and often even—
motivational? the warm walking night
                                    wandering
amusement of darkness, lips,
                             and
the light, always in wind. Perhaps
that's it: to clean something. A window?

A True Account of Talking to the Sun at Fire Island

The Sun woke me this morning loud
and clear, saying "Hey! I've been
trying to wake you up for fifteen
minutes. Don't be so rude, you are
only the second poet I've ever chosen
to speak to personally
                              so why
aren't you more attentive? If I could
burn you through the window I would
to wake you up. I can't hang around
here all day."
                    "Sorry, Sun, I stayed
up late last night talking to Hal."

"When I woke up Mayakovsky he was
a lot more prompt" the Sun said
petulantly. "Most people are up
already waiting to see if I'm going
to put in an appearance."
                                I tried
to apologize "I missed you yesterday."
"That's better" he said. "I didn't
know you'd come out." "You may be
wondering why I've come so close?"
"Yes" I said beginning to feel hot
wondering if maybe he wasn't burning me
anyway.
            "Frankly I wanted to tell you
I like your poetry. I see a lot
on my rounds and you're okay. You may
not be the greatest thing on earth, but
you're different. Now, I've heard some
say you're crazy, they being excessively
calm themselves to my mind, and other
crazy poets think that you're a boring
reactionary. Not me.
                            Just keep on
like I do and pay no attention. You'll
find that people always will complain
about the atmosphere, either too hot
or too cold too bright or too dark, days

too short or too long.
                    If you don't appear
at all one day they think you're lazy
or dead. Just keep right on, I like it.

And don't worry about your lineage
poetic or natural. The Sun shines on
the jungle, you know, on the tundra
the sea, the ghetto. Wherever you were
I knew it and saw you moving. I was waiting
for you to get to work.

                    And now that you
are making your own days, so to speak,
even if no one reads you but me
you won't be depressed. Not
everyone can look up, even at me. It
hurts their eyes."
                    "Oh Sun, I'm so grateful to you!"

"Thanks and remember I'm watching. It's
easier for me to speak to you out
here. I don't have to slide down
between buildings to get your ear.
I know you love Manhattan, but
you ought to look up more often.
                              And
always embrace things, people earth
sky stars, as I do, freely and with
the appropriate sense of space. That
is your inclination, known in the heavens
and you should follow it to hell, if
necessary, which I doubt.
                    Maybe we'll
speak again in Africa, of which I too
am specially fond. Go back to sleep now
Frank, and I may leave a tiny poem
in that brain of yours as my farewell."

"Sun, don't go!" I was awake
at last. "No, go I must, they're calling
me."
    "Who are they?"
                    Rising he said "Some
day you'll know. They're calling to you
too." Darkly he rose, and then I slept.

To Gottfried Benn

Poetry is not instruments
that work at times
then walk out on you
laugh at you old
get drunk on you young
poetry's part of your self

like the passion of a nation
at war it moves quickly
provoked to defense or aggression
unreasoning power
an instinct for self-declaration

like nations its faults are absorbed
in the heat of sides and angles
combatting the void of rounds
a solid of imperfect placement
nations get worse and worse

but not wrongly revealed
in the universal light of tragedy

The Day Lady Died

It is 12:20 in New York a Friday
three days after Bastille day, yes
it is 1959 and I go get a shoeshine
because I will get off the 4:19 in Easthampton
at 7:15 and then go straight to dinner
and I don't know the people who will feed me

I walk up the muggy street beginning to sun
and have a hamburger and a malted and buy
an ugly NEW WORLD WRITING to see what the poets
in Ghana are doing these days
                                            I go on to the bank
and Miss Stillwagon (first name Linda I once heard)
doesn't even look up my balance for once in her life
and in the GOLDEN GRIFFIN I get a little Verlaine
for Patsy with drawings by Bonnard although I do
think of Hesiod, trans. Richmond Lattimore or
Brendan Behan's new play or *Le Balcon* or *Les Nègres*
of Genet, but I don't, I stick with Verlaine
after practically going to sleep with quandariness

and for Mike I just stroll into the PARK LANE
Liquor Store and ask for a bottle of Strega and
then I go back where I came from to 6th Avenue
and the tobacconist in the Ziegfeld Theatre and
casually ask for a carton of Gauloises and a carton
of Picayunes, and a NEW YORK POST with her face on it

and I am sweating a lot by now and thinking of
leaning on the john door in the 5 SPOT
while she whispered a song along the keyboard
to Mal Waldron and everyone and I stopped breathing

Adieu to Norman, Bon Jour to Joan and Jean-Paul

It is 12:10 in New York and I am wondering
if I will finish this in time to meet Norman for lunch
ah lunch! I think I am going crazy
what with my terrible hangover and the weekend coming up
at excitement-prone Kenneth Koch's
I wish I were staying in town and working on my poems
at Joan's studio for a new book by Grove Press
which they will probably not print
but it is good to be several floors up in the dead of night
wondering whether you are any good or not
and the only decision you can make is that you did it

yesterday I looked up the rue Frémicourt on a map
and was happy to find it like a bird
flying over Paris et ses environs
which unfortunately did not include Seine-et-Oise which I don't know
as well as a number of other things
and Allen is back talking about god a lot
and Peter is back not talking very much
and Joe has a cold and is not coming to Kenneth's
although he is coming to lunch with Norman
I suspect he is making a distinction
well, who isn't

I wish I were reeling around Paris
instead of reeling around New York
I wish I weren't reeling at all
it is Spring the ice has melted the Ricard is being poured
we are all happy and young and toothless
it is the same as old age
the only thing to do is simply continue
is that simple
yes, it is simple because it is the only thing to do
can you do it
yes, you can because it is the only thing to do
blue light over the Bois de Boulogne it continues
the Seine continues
the Louvre stays open it continues it hardly closes at all
the Bar Américain continues to be French
de Gaulle continues to be Algerian as does Camus

Shirley Goldfarb continues to be Shirley Goldfarb
and Jane Hazan continues to be Jane Freilicher (I think!)
and Irving Sandler continues to be the balayeur des artistes
and so do I (sometimes I think I'm "in love" with painting)
and surely the Piscine Deligny continues to have water in it
and the Flore continues to have tables and newspapers and people under them
and surely we shall not continue to be unhappy
we shall be happy
but we shall continue to be ourselves everything continues to be possible
René Char, Pierre Reverdy, Samuel Beckett it is possible isn't it
I love Reverdy for saying yes, though I don't believe it

Joe's Jacket

Entraining to Southampton in the parlor car with Jap and Vincent, I
see life as a penetrable landscape lit from above
like it was in my Barbizonian kiddy days when automobiles
were owned by the same people for years and the Alfa Romeo was
only a rumor under the leaves beside the viaduct and I
pretending to be adult felt the blue within me and the light up there
no central figure me, I was some sort of cloud or a gust of wind
at the station a crowd of drunken fishermen on a picnic Kenneth
is hard to find but we find, through all the singing, Kenneth smiling
it is off to Janice's bluefish and the incessant talk of affection
expressed as excitability and spleen to be recent and strong
and not unbearably right in attitude, full of confidences
now I will say it, thank god, I knew you would

an enormous party mesmerizing comers in the disgathering light
and dancing miniature-endless like a pivot
I drink to smother my sensitivity for a while so I won't stare away
I drink to kill the fear of boredom, the mounting panic of it
I drink to reduce my seriousness so a certain spurious charm
can appear and win its flickering little victory over noise
I drink to die a little and increase the contrast of this questionable moment
and then I am going home, purged of everything except anxiety and self-distrust
now I will say it, thank god, I knew you would
and the rain has commenced its delicate lament over the orchards

an enormous window morning and the wind, the beautiful desperation of a tree
fighting off strangulation, and my bed has an ugly calm
I reach to the D.H. Lawrence on the floor and read "The Ship of Death"
I lie back again and begin slowly to drift and then to sink
a somnolent envy of inertia makes me rise naked and go to the window
where the car horn mysteriously starts to honk, no one is there
and Kenneth comes out and stops it in the soft green lightless stare
and we are soon in the Paris of Kenneth's libretto, I did not drift
away I did not die I am there with Haussmann and the rue de Rivoli
and the spirits of beauty, art and progress, pertinent and mobile
in their worldly way, and musical and strange the sun comes out

returning by car the forceful histories of myself and Vincent loom
like the city hour after hour closer and closer to the future I am here
and the night is heavy though not warm, Joe is still up and we talk

only of the immediate present and its indiscriminately hitched-to past
the feeling of life and incident pouring over the sleeping city
which seems to be bathed in an unobtrusive light which lends things
coherence and an absolute, for just that time as four o'clock goes by

and soon I am rising for the less than average day, I have coffee
I prepare calmly to face almost everything that will come up I am calm
but not as my bed was calm as it softly declined to become a ship
I borrow Joe's seersucker jacket though he is still asleep I start out
when I last borrowed it I was leaving there it was on my Spanish plaza back
and hid my shoulders from San Marco's pigeons was jostled on the
     Kurfürstendamm
and sat opposite Ashes in an enormous leather chair in the Continental
it is all enormity and life it has protected me and kept me here on
many occasions as a symbol does when the heart is full and risks no speech
a precaution I loathe as the pheasant loathes the season and is preserved
it will not be need, it will be just what it is and just what happens

You Are Gorgeous and I'm Coming

Vaguely I hear the purple roar of the torn-down Third Avenue El
it sways slightly but firmly like a hand or a golden-downed thigh
normally I don't think of sounds as colored unless I'm feeling corrupt
concrete Rimbaud obscurity of emotion which is simple and very definite
even lasting, yes it may be that dark and purifying wave, the death of boredom
nearing the heights themselves may destroy you in the pure air
to be further complicated, confused, empty but refilling, exposed to light

With the past falling away as an acceleration of nerves thundering and shaking
aims its aggregating force like the Métro towards a realm of encircling travel
rending the sound of adventure and becoming ultimately local and intimate
repeating the phrases of an old romance which is constantly renewed by the
endless originality of human loss the air the stumbling quiet of breathing
newly the heavens' stars all out we are all for the captured time of our being

Poem

Khrushchev is coming on the right day!
                                        the cool graced light
is pushed off the enormous glass piers by hard wind
and everything is tossing, hurrying on up
                                        this country
has everything but *politesse*, a Puerto Rican cab driver says
and five different girls I see
                                look like Piedie Gimbel
with her blonde hair tossing too,
                                        as she looked when I pushed
her little daughter on the swing on the lawn it was also windy

last night we went to a movie and came out,
                                        Ionesco is greater
than Beckett, Vincent said, that's what I think, blueberry blintzes
and Khrushchev was probably being carped at
                                in Washington, no *politesse*
Vincent tells me about his mother's trip to Sweden
                                        Hans tells us
about his father's life in Sweden, it sounds like Grace Hartigan's
painting *Sweden*
                so I go home to bed and names drift through my head
Purgatorio Merchado, Gerhard Schwartz and Gaspar Gonzales, all
                unknown figures of the early morning as I go to work

where does the evil of the year go
                                when September takes New York
and turns it into ozone stalagmites
                                deposits of light
                                so I get back up
make coffee, and read François Villon, his life, so dark
        New York seems blinding and my tie is blowing up the street
I wish it would blow off
                        though it is cold and somewhat warms my neck
as the train bears Khrushchev on to Pennsylvania Station
        and the light seems to be eternal
        and joy seems to be inexorable
        I am foolish enough always to find it in wind

Getting Up Ahead of Someone (Sun)

I cough a lot (sinus?) so I
get up and have some tea with cognac
it is dawn
        the light flows evenly along the lawn
in chilly Southampton and I smoke
and hours and hours go by I read
van Vechten's *Spider Boy* then a short
story by Patsy Southgate and a poem
by myself it is cold and I shiver a little
in white shorts the day begun
so oddly not tired not nervous I
am for once truly awake letting it all
start slowly as I watch instead of
grabbing on late as usual
                where did it go
                it's not really awake yet
                I will wait

and the house wakes up and goes
to get the dog in Sag Harbor I make
myself a bourbon and commence
to write one of my "I do this I do that"
poems in a sketch pad
                it is tomorrow
though only six hours have gone by
each day's light has more significance these days

Steps

How funny you are today New York
like Ginger Rogers in *Swingtime*
and St. Bridget's steeple leaning a little to the left

here I have just jumped out of a bed full of V-days
(I got tired of D-days) and blue you there still
accepts me foolish and free
all I want is a room up there
and you in it
and even the traffic halt so thick is a way
for people to rub up against each other
and when their surgical appliances lock
they stay together
for the rest of the day (what a day)
I go by to check a slide and I say
that painting's not so blue

where's Lana Turner
she's out eating
and Garbo's backstage at the Met
everyone's taking their coat off
so they can show a rib-cage to the rib-watchers
and the park's full of dancers with their tights and shoes
in little bags
who are often mistaken for worker-outers at the West Side Y
why not
the Pittsburgh Pirates shout because they won
and in a sense we're all winning
we're alive

the apartment was vacated by a gay couple
who moved to the country for fun
they moved a day too soon
even the stabbings are helping the population explosion
though in the wrong country
and all those liars have left the UN
the Seagram Building's no longer rivalled in interest
not that we need liquor (we just like it)

and the little box is out on the sidewalk
next to the delicatessen
so the old man can sit on it and drink beer
and get knocked off it by his wife later in the day
while the sun is still shining

oh god it's wonderful
to get out of bed
and drink too much coffee
and smoke too many cigarettes
and love you so much

Ave Maria

Mothers of America
                  let your kids go to the movies!
get them out of the house so they won't know what you're up to
it's true that fresh air is good for the body
                                 but what about the soul
that grows in darkness, embossed by silvery images
and when you grow old as grow old you must
                                 they won't hate you
they won't criticize you they won't know
                            they'll be in some glamorous country
they first saw on a Saturday afternoon or playing hookey

they may even be grateful to you
                        for their first sexual experience
which only cost you a quarter
                        and didn't upset the peaceful home
they will know where candy bars come from
                              and gratuitous bags of popcorn
as gratuitous as leaving the movie before it's over
with a pleasant stranger whose apartment is in the Heaven on Earth Bldg
near the Williamsburg Bridge
                      oh mothers you will have made the little tykes
so happy because if nobody does pick them up in the movies
they won't know the difference
                      and if somebody does it'll be sheer gravy
and they'll have been truly entertained either way
instead of hanging around the yard
                    or up in their room
                            hating you
prematurely since you won't have done anything horribly mean yet
except keeping them from the darker joys
                        it's unforgivable the latter
so don't blame me if you won't take this advice
                        and the family breaks up
and your children grow old and blind in front of a TV set
                          seeing
movies you wouldn't let them see when they were young

Poem

Lana Turner has collapsed!
I was trotting along and suddenly
it started raining and snowing
and you said it was hailing
but hailing hits you on the head
hard so it was really snowing and
raining and I was in such a hurry
to meet you but the traffic
was acting exactly like the sky
and suddenly I see a headline
LANA TURNER HAS COLLAPSED!
there is no snow in Hollywood
there is no rain in California
I have been to lots of parties
and acted perfectly disgraceful
but I never actually collapsed
oh Lana Turner we love you get up

First Dances

1

From behind he takes her waist
and lifts her, her lavender waist
stained with tears and her mascara
is running, her neck is tired
from drooping. She floats she steps
automatically correct, then suddenly
she is alive up there and smiles.
How much greater triumph for him
that she had so despaired when his
hands encircled her like a pillar
and lifted her into the air
which after him will turn to rock-
like boredom, but not till after
many hims and he will not be there.

2

The punch bowl was near the cloakroom
so the pints could be taken out of the
boys' cloaks and dumped into the punch.
Outside the branches beat hysterically
towards the chandeliers, just fended
off by fearful windows. The chandeliers
giggle a little. There were many
introductions but few invitations. I
found a spot of paint on my coat as
others found pimples. It is easy to
dance it is even easy to dance together
sometimes. We were very young and ugly
we knew it, everybody knew it.

3

A white hall inside a church. Nerves.

Fantasy

dedicated to the health of Allen Ginsberg

How do you like the music of Adolph
                              Deutsch? I like
it, I like it better than Max Steiner's. Take his
score for *Northern Pursuit*, the Helmut Dantine theme
was . . .
              and then the window fell on my hand. Errol
Flynn was skiing by. Down
                              down down went the grim
gray submarine under the "cold" ice.
                              Helmut was
safely ashore, on the ice.
                              What dreams, what incredible
fantasies of snow farts will this all lead to?
                                                  I
don't know, I have stopped thinking like a sled dog.

The main thing is to tell a story.
                              It is almost
very important. Imagine
                              throwing away the avalanche
so early in the movie. I am the only spy left
in Canada,
              but just because I'm alone in the snow
doesn't necessarily mean I'm a Nazi.
                              Let's see,
two aspirins a vitamin C tablet and some baking soda
should do the trick, that's practically an
                                                  Alka
Seltzer. Allen come out of the bathroom
                              and take it.
I think someone put butter on my skis instead
of wax.
              Ouch. The leanto is falling over in the
firs, and there is another fatter spy here. They
didn't tell me they sent
                              him. Well, that takes care
of him, boy were those huskies hungry.
                              Allen,

are you feeling any better? Yes, I'm crazy about
Helmut Dantine
                    but I'm glad that Canada will remain
free. Just free, that's all, never argue with the movies.

John Ashbery

JOHN ASHBERY

John Ashbery was born in Rochester in 1927, and grew up on a farm near Sodus. He went to schools in Rochester and Sodus, but then at the age of sixteen was sent as a boarder to Deerfield Academy in Massachusetts. He entered Harvard University in 1945, and, with the support of Kenneth Koch, was elected to the board of the *Advocate*. While still an undergraduate he composed the sestina, 'The Painter' and what would be the title poem of his first collection, 'Some Trees'. Ashbery moved to New York in 1949, where he studied for an MA in English Literature at Columbia University, submitting a thesis on the novels of Henry Green. On graduating he spent several years working in publishing in New York, but in 1955 was awarded a Fulbright fellowship, which took him first to Montpellier, and then to Rennes and Paris. *Some Trees* appeared the following year, having been selected by W.H. Auden for the Yale Younger Poets Award.

Ashbery was to spend most of the next ten years in Paris. He intended to write a doctoral dissertation on the work of Raymond Roussel, but despite undertaking much preliminary investigative research, this project was never completed. He supported himself with translation work, and as Paris art critic for the international edition of *The New York Herald Tribune*. His second collection, *The Tennis Court Oath*, was published in 1962, and contains some of his most experimental and fragmented works. He began putting poetry 'back together again' in his third collection, *Rivers and Mountains* (1966), the bulk of which consists of a single long poem, 'The Skaters', initially inspired by an English Edwardian book for children called *Three Hundred Things a Bright Boy Can Do* that he had bought from a second-hand book stall on the banks of the Seine. The long lines of 'The Skaters' reveal Ashbery at his most Whitmanesque, intercutting memories of a lonely, snow-bound childhood with teasingly evasive reflections on his *ars poetica*: 'I am not ready', he writes in Part I of the poem, 'to line phrases with the costly stuff of explanation, and shall not, / Will not do so for the moment.'

In November 1965 Ashbery returned to New York, where he took up the post of executive editor for *Art News*. His 1970 collection, *The Double Dream of Spring* – its title is borrowed from a painting by one of his favourite artists, Giorgio de

Chirico – contains what has become his most anthologised poem, 'Soonest Mended', which he once described as a 'one-size-fits-all Confessional poem'. His work had by this time attracted the attention of a wide range of poetry critics, including David Kalstone, Marjorie Perloff, Richard Howard, and Harold Bloom, whose influential study, *The Anxiety of Influence*, published in 1973, concludes with a chapter on Ashbery. Two years later, *Self-Portrait in a Convex Mirror* was awarded all three of America's most prestigious poetry prizes: the Pulitzer, the National Book Award, and the National Book Critics' Circle Award. The volume's long title poem, a meditation on Parmigianino's extraordinary hemispherical self-portrait of 1524, explores, like 'The Skaters', the contradictions inherent in the impulse to compose a song of one's self. The poem almost immediately generated numerous critical interpretations, and Ashbery has now become one of the most written about poets of the post-war era.

He was by this time himself teaching in a university. *Art News* was sold in 1972, and the entire staff sacked. Ashbery accepted a job at Brooklyn College, though he continued to review exhibitions for magazines such as *New York* and *Newsweek*. A selection of his art criticism, edited by David Bergman, appeared under the title *Reported Sightings* in 1989. Ashbery has published one other volume of critical prose, *Other Traditions* (2000), which consists of essays, based on his Charles Eliot Norton lectures of 1989–90, about six writers whose work he has found particularly inspiring: John Clare, Thomas Lovell Beddoes, Raymond Roussel, Laura Riding, David Schubert, and John Wheelwright.

Perhaps the most exhilarating aspect of Ashbery's poetic career has been his continual determination to experiment. His work makes use of a dazzling range of forms, dictions, and registers. His poems demonstrate an unnerving, but ultimately liberating, ability to assimilate diverse kinds of experience, as they glide from the sublime to the bathetic to the surreal to the lyrical, by turns comic and desperate in their examination of the means by which we make sense of our lives.

The Picture of Little J.A. in a Prospect of Flowers

He was spoilt from childhood by the future, which he mastered rather early and apparently without great difficulty.

Boris Pasternak

I

Darkness falls like a wet sponge
And Dick gives Genevieve a swift punch
In the pajamas. "Aroint thee, witch."
Her tongue from previous ecstasy
Releases thoughts like little hats.

"He clap'd me first during the eclipse.
Afterwards I noted his manner
Much altered. But he sending
At that time certain handsome jewels
I durst not seem to take offence."

In a far recess of summer
Monks are playing soccer.

II

So far is goodness a mere memory
Or naming of recent scenes of badness
That even these lives, children,
You may pass through to be blessed,
So fair does each invent his virtue.

And coming from a white world, music
Will sparkle at the lips of many who are
Beloved. Then these, as dirty handmaidens
To some transparent witch, will dream
Of a white hero's subtle wooing,
And time shall force a gift on each.

That beggar to whom you gave no cent
Striped the night with his strange descant.

III

Yet I cannot escape the picture
Of my small self in that bank of flowers:
My head among the blazing phlox
Seemed a pale and gigantic fungus.
I had a hard stare, accepting

Everything, taking nothing,
As though the rolled-up future might stink
As loud as stood the sick moment
The shutter clicked. Though I was wrong,
Still, as the loveliest feelings

Must soon find words, and these, yes,
Displace them, so I am not wrong
In calling this comic version of myself
The true one. For as change is horror,
Virtue is really stubbornness

And only in the light of lost words
Can we imagine our rewards.

Some Trees

These are amazing: each
Joining a neighbor, as though speech
Were a still performance.
Arranging by chance

To meet as far this morning
From the world as agreeing
With it, you and I
Are suddenly what the trees try

To tell us we are:
That their merely being there
Means something; that soon
We may touch, love, explain.

And glad not to have invented
Such comeliness, we are surrounded:
A silence already filled with noises,
A canvas on which emerges

A chorus of smiles, a winter morning.
Placed in a puzzling light, and moving,
Our days put on such reticence
These accents seem their own defense.

The Painter

Sitting between the sea and the buildings
He enjoyed painting the sea's portrait.
But just as children imagine a prayer
Is merely silence, he expected his subject
To rush up the sand, and, seizing a brush,
Plaster its own portrait on the canvas.

So there was never any paint on his canvas
Until the people who lived in the buildings
Put him to work: "Try using the brush
As a means to an end. Select, for a portrait,
Something less angry and large, and more subject
To a painter's moods, or, perhaps, to a prayer."

How could he explain to them his prayer
That nature, not art, might usurp the canvas?
He chose his wife for a new subject,
Making her vast, like ruined buildings,
As if, forgetting itself, the portrait
Had expressed itself without a brush.

Slightly encouraged, he dipped his brush
In the sea, murmuring a heartfelt prayer:
"My soul, when I paint this next portrait
Let it be you who wrecks the canvas."
The news spread like wildfire through the buildings:
He had gone back to the sea for his subject.

Imagine a painter crucified by his subject!
Too exhausted even to lift his brush,
He provoked some artists leaning from the buildings
To malicious mirth: "We haven't a prayer
Now, of putting ourselves on canvas,
Or getting the sea to sit for a portrait!"

Others declared it a self-portrait.
Finally all indications of a subject
Began to fade, leaving the canvas
Perfectly white. He put down the brush.
At once a howl, that was also a prayer,
Arose from the overcrowded buildings.

They tossed him, the portrait, from the tallest of the buildings;
And the sea devoured the canvas and the brush
As though his subject had decided to remain a prayer.

"They Dream Only of America"

They dream only of America
To be lost among the thirteen million pillars of grass:
"This honey is delicious
Though it burns the throat."

And hiding from darkness in barns
They can be grownups now
And the murderer's ash tray is more easily—
The lake a lilac cube.

He holds a key in his right hand.
"Please," he asked willingly.
He is thirty years old.
That was before

We could drive hundreds of miles
At night through dandelions.
When his headache grew worse we
Stopped at a wire filling station.

Now he cared only about signs.
Was the cigar a sign?
And what about the key?
He went slowly into the bedroom.

"I would not have broken my leg if I had not fallen
Against the living room table. What is it to be back
Beside the bed? There is nothing to do
For our liberation, except wait in the horror of it.

And I am lost without you."

A Last World

These wonderful things
Were planted on the surface of a round mind that was to become our present
    time.
The mark of things belongs to someone
But if that somebody was wise
Then the whole of things might be different
From what it was thought to be in the beginning, before an angel bandaged the
    field glasses.
Then one could say nothing hear nothing
Of what the great time spoke to its divisors.
All borders between men were closed.
Now all is different without having changed
As though one were to pass through the same street at different times
And nothing that is old can prefer the new.
An enormous merit has been placed on the head of all things
Which, bowing down, arrive near the region of their feet
So that the earth-stone has stared at them in memory at the approach of an error.
Still it is not too late for these things to die
Provided that an anemone will grab them and rush them to the wildest heaven.
But having plucked oneself, who could live in the sunlight?
And the truth is cold, as a giant's knee
Will seem cold.

Yet having once played with tawny truth
Having once looked at a cold mullet on a plate on a table supported by the
    weight of the inconstant universe
He wished to go far away from himself.
There were no baskets in those jovial pine-tree forests, and the waves pushed
    without whitecaps
In that foam where he wished to be.

Man is never without woman, the neuter sex
Casting up her equations, looks to her lord for loving kindness
For man smiles never at woman.
In the forests a night landslide could disclose that she smiled.
Guns were fired to discourage dogs into the interior
But woman—never. She is completely out of this world.
She climbs a tree to see if he is coming
Sunlight breaks at the edges of the wet lakes
And she is happy, if free
For the power he forces down at her like a storm of lightning.

Once a happy old man
One can never change the core of things, and light burns you the harder for it.
Glad of the changes already and if there are more it will never be you that minds
Since it will not be you to be changed, but in the evening in the severe lamp-
     light doubts come
From many scattered distances, and do not come too near.
As it falls along the house, your treasure
Cries to the other men; the darkness will have none of you, and you are folded
     into it like mint into the sound of haying.
It was ninety-five years ago that you strolled in the serene little port; under an
     enormous cornice six boys in black slowly stood.
Six frock coats today, six black fungi tomorrow,
And the day after tomorrow—but the day after tomorrow itself is blackening
     dust.
You court obsidian pools
And from a tremendous height twilight falls like a stone and hits you.
You who were always in the way
Flower
Are you afraid of trembling like breath
But there is no breath in seriousness; the lake howls for it.
Swiftly sky covers earth, the wrong breast for a child to suck, and that,
What have you got there in your hand?
It is a stone

So the passions are divided into tiniest units
And of these many are lost, and those that remain are given at nightfall to the
     uneasy old man
The old man who goes skipping along the roadbed.
In a dumb harvest
Passions are locked away, and states of creation are used instead, that is to say
     synonyms are used.

Honey
On the lips of elders is not contenting, so
A firebrand is made. Woman carries it,
She who thought herself good only for bearing children is decked out in the
     lace of fire
And this is exactly the way she wanted it, the trees coming to place themselves
     in her
In a rite of torpor, dust.
A bug carries the elixir
Naked men pray the ground and chew it with their hands
The fire lives

Men are nabbed
She her bonnet half off is sobbing there while the massacre yet continues with a
    terrific thin energy
A silver blaze calms the darkness.

Rest undisturbed on the dry of the beach
Flower
And night stand suddenly sideways to observe your bones
Vixen

Do men later go home
Because we wanted to travel
Under the kettle of trees
We thought the sky would melt to see us
But to tell the truth the air turned to smoke,
We were forced back onto a foul pillow that was another place.
Or were lost by our comrades
Somewhere between heaven and no place, and were growing smaller.
In another place a mysterious mist shot up like a wall, down which trickled the
    tears of our loved ones.
Bananas rotten with their ripeness hung from the leaves, and cakes and jewels
    covered the sand.
But these were not the best men
But there were moments of the others
Seen through indifference, only bare methods
But we can remember them and so we are saved.

A last world moves on the figures;
They are smaller than when we last saw them caring about them.
The sky is a giant rocking horse
And of the other things death is a new office building filled with modern
    furniture,
A wise thing, but which has no purpose for us.

Everything is being blown away;
A little horse trots up with a letter in its mouth, which is read with eagerness
As we gallop into the flame.

These Lacustrine Cities

These lacustrine cities grew out of loathing
Into something forgetful, although angry with history.
They are the product of an idea: that man is horrible, for instance,
Though this is only one example.

They emerged until a tower
Controlled the sky, and with artifice dipped back
Into the past for swans and tapering branches,
Burning, until all that hate was transformed into useless love.

Then you are left with an idea of yourself
And the feeling of ascending emptiness of the afternoon
Which must be charged to the embarrassment of others
Who fly by you like beacons.

The night is a sentinel.
Much of your time has been occupied by creative games
Until now, but we have all-inclusive plans for you.
We had thought, for instance, of sending you to the middle of the desert,

To a violent sea, or of having the closeness of the others be air
To you, pressing you back into a startled dream
As sea-breezes greet a child's face.
But the past is already here, and you are nursing some private project.

The worst is not over, yet I know
You will be happy here. Because of the logic
Of your situation, which is something no climate can outsmart.
Tender and insouciant by turns, you see

You have built a mountain of something,
Thoughtfully pouring all your energy into this single monument,
Whose wind is desire starching a petal,
Whose disappointment broke into a rainbow of tears.

from *The Skaters*

1

These decibels
Are a kind of flagellation, an entity of sound
Into which being enters, and is apart.
Their colors on a warm February day
Make for masses of inertia, and hips
Prod out of the violet-seeming into a new kind
Of demand that stumps the absolute because not new
In the sense of the next one in an infinite series
But, as it were, pre-existing or pre-seeming in
Such a way as to contrast funnily with the unexpectedness
And somehow push us all into perdition.

Here a scarf flies, there an excited call is heard.

The answer is that it is novelty
That guides these swift blades o'er the ice,
Projects into a finer expression (but at the expense
Of energy) the profile I cannot remember.
Colors slip away from and chide us. The human mind
Cannot retain anything except perhaps the dismal two-note theme
Of some sodden "dump" or lament.

But the water surface ripples, the whole light changes.

We children are ashamed of our bodies
But we laugh and, demanded, talk of sex again
And all is well. The waves of morning harshness
Float away like coal-gas into the sky.
But how much survives? How much of any one of us survives?
The articles we'd collect—stamps of the colonies
With greasy cancellation marks, mauve, magenta and chocolate,
Or funny-looking dogs we'd see in the street, or bright remarks.
One collects bullets. An Indianapolis, Indiana man collects slingshots of all
    epochs, and so on.

Subtracted from our collections, though, these go on a little while, collecting
    aimlessly. We still support them.
But so little energy they have! And up the swollen sands

Staggers the darkness fiend, with the storm fiend close behind him!
True, melodious tolling does go on in that awful pandemonium,
Certain resonances are not utterly displeasing to the terrified eardrum.
Some paroxysms are dinning of tambourine, others suggest piano room or
    organ loft
For the most dissonant night charms us, even after death. This, after all, may be
    happiness: tuba notes awash on the great flood, ruptures of xylophone,
    violins, limpets, grace-notes, the musical instrument called serpent, viola
    da gambas, aeolian harps, clavicles, pinball machines, electric drills, *que*
    sais-je encore!
The performance has rapidly reached your ear; silent and tear-stained, in the
    post-mortem shock, you stand listening, awash
With memories of hair in particular, part of the welling that is you,
The gurgling of harp, cymbal, glockenspiel, triangle, temple block, English
    horn and metronome! And still no presentiment, no feeling of pain before
    or after.
The passage sustains, does not give. And you have come far indeed.

Yet to go from "not interesting" to "old and uninteresting,"
To be surrounded by friends, though late in life,
To hear the wings of the spirit, though far. . . .
Why do I hurriedly undrown myself to cut you down?
"I am yesterday," and my fault is eternal.
I do not expect constant attendance, knowing myself insufficient for your
    present demands
And I have a dim intuition that I am that other "I" with which we began.
My cheeks as blank walls to your tears and eagerness
Fondling that other, as though you had let him get away forever.

The evidence of the visual henceforth replaced
By the great shadow of trees falling over life.

A child's devotion
To this normal, shapeless entity. . . .

Forgotten as the words fly briskly across, each time
Bringing down meaning as snow from a low sky, or rabbits flushed from a wood.
How strange that the narrow perspective lines
Always seem to meet, although parallel, and that an insane ghost could do this,
Could make the house seem so much farther in the distance, as
It seemed to the horse, dragging the sledge of a perspective line.
Dim banners in the distance, to die. . . . And nothing put to rights. The pigs in
    their cages

And so much snow, but it is to be littered with waste and ashes
So that cathedrals may grow. Out of this spring builds a tolerable
Affair of brushwood, the sea is felt behind oak wands, noiselessly pouring.
Spring with its promise of winter, and the black ivy once again
On the porch, its yellow perspective bands in place
And the horse nears them and weeps.

So much has passed through my mind this morning
That I can give you but a dim account of it:
It is already after lunch, the men are returning to their positions around the
    cement mixer
And I try to sort out what has happened to me. The bundle of Gerard's letters,
And that awful bit of news buried on the back page of yesterday's paper.
Then the news of you this morning, in the snow. Sometimes the interval
Of bad news is so brisk that . . . And the human brain, with its tray of images
Seems a sorcerer's magic lantern, projecting black and orange cellophane
    shadows
On the distance of my hand . . . The very reaction's puny,
And when we seek to move around, wondering what our position is now,
    what the arm of that chair.

A great wind lifted these cardboard panels
Horizontal in the air. At once the perspective with the horse
Disappeared in a *bigarrure* of squiggly lines. The image with the crocodile in it
    became no longer apparent.
Thus a great wind cleanses, as a new ruler
Edits new laws, sweeping the very breath of the streets
Into posterior trash. The films have changed—
The great titles on the scalloped awning have turned dry and blight-colored.
No wind that does not penetrate a man's house, into the very bowels of the
    furnace,
Scratching in dust a name on the mirror—say, and what about letters,
The dried grasses, fruits of the winter—gosh! Everything is trash!
The wind points to the advantages of decay
At the same time as removing them far from the sight of men.
The regent of the winds, Aeolus, is a symbol for all earthly potentates
Since holding this sickening, festering process by which we are cleansed
Of afterthought.
           A girl slowly descended the line of steps.

The wind and treason are partners, turning secrets over to the military police.

Lengthening arches. The intensity of minor acts. As skaters elaborate their
        distances,
Taking a separate line to its end. Returning to the mass, they join each other
Blotted in an incredible mess of dark colors, and again reappearing to take the
        theme
Some little distance, like fishing boats developing from the land different
        parabolas,
Taking the exquisite theme far, into farness, to Land's End, to the ends of the
        earth!

But the livery of the year, the changing air
Bring each to fulfillment. Leaving phrases unfinished,
Gestures half-sketched against woodsmoke. The abundant sap
Oozes in girls' throats, the sticky words, half-uttered, unwished for,
A blanket disbelief, quickly supplanted by idle questions that fade in turn.
Slowly the mood turns to look at itself as some urchin
Forgotten by the roadside. New schemes are got up, new taxes,
Earthworks. And the hours becomes light again.
Girls wake up in it.

It is best to remain indoors. Because there is error
In so much precision. As flames are fanned, wishful thinking arises
Bearing its own prophets, its pointed ignoring. And just as a desire
Settles down at the end of a long spring day, over heather and watered shoot
        and dried rush field,
So error is plaited into desires not yet born.

Therefore the post must be resumed (is being falsified
To be forever involved, tragically, with one's own image?).
The studio light suddenly invaded the long casement—values were what
She knows now. But the floor is being slowly pulled apart
Like straw under those limpid feet.
And Helga, in the minuscule apartment in Jersey City
Is reacting violet to the same kind of dress, is drawing death
Again in blossoms against the reactionary fire . . . pulsing
And knowing nothing to superb lambent distances that intercalate
This city. Is the death of the cube repeated. Or in the musical album.

It is time now for a general understanding of
The meaning of all this. The meaning of Helga, importance of the setting, etc.
A description of the blues. Labels on bottles
And all kinds of discarded objects that ought to be described.
But can one ever be sure of which ones?

Isn't this a death-trap, wanting to put too much in
So the floor sags, as under the weight of a piano, or a piano-legged girl
And the whole house of cards comes dinning down around one's ears!
But this is an important aspect of the question
Which I am not ready to discuss, am not at all ready to,
This leaving-out business. On it hinges the very importance of what's novel
Or autocratic, or dense or silly. It is as well to call attention
To it by exaggeration, perhaps. But calling attention
Isn't the same thing as explaining, and as I said I am not ready
To line phrases with the costly stuff of explanation, and shall not,
Will not do so for the moment. Except to say that the carnivorous
Way of these lines is to devour their own nature, leaving
Nothing but a bitter impression of absence, which as we know involves
        presence, but still.
Nevertheless these are fundamental absences, struggling to get up and be off
        themselves.

This, thus, is a portion of the subject of this poem
Which is in the form of falling snow:
That is, the individual flakes are not essential to the importance of the whole's
        becoming so much of a truism
That their importance is again called in question, to be denied further out, and
        again and again like this.
Hence, neither the importance of the individual flake,
Nor the importance of the whole impression of the storm, if it has any, is what
        it is,
But the rhythm of the series of repeated jumps, from abstract into positive and
        back to a slightly less diluted abstract.

Mild effects are the result.

I cannot think any more of going out into all that, will stay here
With my quiet *schmerzen*. Besides the storm is almost over
Having frozen the face of the bust into a strange style with the lips
And the teeth the most distinct part of the whole business.

It is this madness to explain. . . .

What is the matter with plain old-fashioned cause-and-effect?
Leaving one alone with romantic impressions of the trees, the sky?
Who, actually, is going to be fooled one instant by these phony explanations,
Think them important? So back we go to the old, imprecise feelings, the
Common knowledge, the importance of duly suffering and the occasional glimpses

Of some balmy felicity. The world of Schubert's lieder. I am fascinated
Though by the urge to get out of it all, by going
Further in and correcting the whole mismanaged mess. But am afraid I'll
Be of no help to you. Good-bye.

As balloons are to the poet, so to the ground
Its varied assortment of trees. The more assorted they are, the
Vaster his experience. Sometimes
You catch sight of them on a level with the top story of a house,
Strung up there for publicity purposes. Or like those bubbles
Children make with a kind of ring, not a pipe, and probably using some
    detergent
Rather than plain everyday soap and water. Where was I? The balloons
Drift thoughtfully over the land, not exactly commenting on it;
These are the range of the poet's experience. He can hide in trees
Like a hamadryad, but wisely prefers not to, letting the balloons
Idle him out of existence, as a car idles. Traveling faster
And more furiously across unknown horizons, belted into the night
Wishing more and more to be unlike someone, getting the whole thing
(So he believes) out of his system. Inventing systems.
We are a part of some system, thinks he, just as the sun is part of
The solar system. Trees brake his approach. And he seems to be wearing but
Half a coat, viewed from one side. A "half-man" look inspiring the disgust of
    honest folk
Returning from chores, the milk frozen, the pump heaped high with a chapeau
    of snow,
The "No Skating" sign as well. But it is here that he is best,
Face to face with the unsmiling alternatives of his nerve-wracking existence.
Placed squarely in front of his dilemma, on all fours before the lamentable
    spectacle of the unknown.
Yet knowing where men are coming from. It is this, to hold the candle up to the
    album.

Soonest Mended

Barely tolerated, living on the margin
In our technological society, we were always having to be rescued
On the brink of destruction, like heroines in *Orlando Furioso*
Before it was time to start all over again.
There would be thunder in the bushes, a rustling of coils,
And Angelica, in the Ingres painting, was considering
The colorful but small monster near her toe, as though wondering whether
    forgetting
The whole thing might not, in the end, be the only solution.
And then there always came a time when
Happy Hooligan in his rusted green automobile
Came plowing down the course, just to make sure everything was O.K.,
Only by that time we were in another chapter and confused
About how to receive this latest piece of information.
Was it information? Weren't we rather acting this out
For someone else's benefit, thoughts in a mind
With room enough and to spare for our little problems (so they began to seem),
Our daily quandary about food and the rent and bills to be paid?
To reduce all this to a small variant,
To step free at last, minuscule on the gigantic plateau—
This was our ambition: to be small and clear and free.
Alas, the summer's energy wanes quickly,
A moment and it is gone. And no longer
May we make the necessary arrangements, simple as they are.
Our star was brighter perhaps when it had water in it.
Now there is no question even of that, but only
Of holding on to the hard earth so as not to get thrown off,
With an occasional dream, a vision: a robin flies across
The upper corner of the window, you brush your hair away
And cannot quite see, or a wound will flash
Against the sweet faces of the others, something like:
This is what you wanted to hear, so why
Did you think of listening to something else? We are all talkers
It is true, but underneath the talk lies
The moving and not wanting to be moved, the loose
Meaning, untidy and simple like a threshing floor.

These then were some hazards of the course,
Yet though we knew the course *was* hazards and nothing else
It was still a shock when, almost a quarter of a century later,

The clarity of the rules dawned on you for the first time.
They were the players, and we who had struggled at the game
Were merely spectators, though subject to its vicissitudes
And moving with it out of the tearful stadium, borne on shoulders, at last.
Night after night this message returns, repeated
In the flickering bulbs of the sky, raised past us, taken away from us,
Yet ours over and over until the end that is past truth,
The being of our sentences, in the climate that fostered them,
Not ours to own, like a book, but to be with, and sometimes
To be without, alone and desperate.
But the fantasy makes it ours, a kind of fence-sitting
Raised to the level of an esthetic ideal. These were moments, years,
Solid with reality, faces, namable events, kisses, heroic acts,
But like the friendly beginning of a geometrical progression
Not too reassuring, as though meaning could be cast aside some day
When it had been outgrown. Better, you said, to stay cowering
Like this in the early lessons, since the promise of learning
Is a delusion, and I agreed, adding that
Tomorrow would alter the sense of what had already been learned,
That the learning process is extended in this way, so that from this standpoint
None of us ever graduates from college,
For time is an emulsion, and probably thinking not to grow up
Is the brightest kind of maturity for us, right now at any rate.
And you see, both of us were right, though nothing
Has somehow come to nothing; the avatars
Of our conforming to the rules and living
Around the home have made—well, in a sense, "good citizens" of us,
Brushing the teeth and all that, and learning to accept
The charity of the hard moments as they are doled out,
For this is action, this not being sure, this careless
Preparing, sowing the seeds crooked in the furrow,
Making ready to forget, and always coming back
To the mooring of starting out, that day so long ago.

Farm Implements and Rutabagas in a Landscape

The first of the undecoded messages read: "Popeye sits in thunder,
Unthought of. From that shoebox of an apartment,
From livid curtain's hue, a tangram emerges: a country."
Meanwhile the Sea Hag was relaxing on a green couch: "How pleasant
To spend one's vacation *en la casa de Popeye*," she scratched
Her cleft chin's solitary hair. She remembered spinach

And was going to ask Wimpy if he had bought any spinach.
"M'love," he intercepted, "the plains are decked out in thunder
Today, and it shall be as you wish." He scratched
The part of his head under his hat. The apartment
Seemed to grow smaller. "But what if no pleasant
Inspiration plunge us now to the stars? *For this is my country.*"

Suddenly they remembered how it was cheaper in the country.
Wimpy was thoughtfully cutting open a number 2 can of spinach
When the door opened and Swee'pea crept in. "How pleasant!"
But Swee'pea looked morose. A note was pinned to his bib. "Thunder
And tears are unavailing," it read. "Henceforth shall Popeye's apartment
Be but remembered space, toxic or salubrious, whole or scratched."

Olive came hurtling through the window; its geraniums scratched
Her long thigh. "I have news!" she gasped. "Popeye, forced as you know to flee
        the country
One musty gusty evening, by the schemes of his wizened, duplicate father,
        jealous of the apartment
And all that it contains, myself and spinach
In particular, heaves bolts of loving thunder
At his own astonished becoming, rupturing the pleasant

Arpeggio of our years. No more shall pleasant
Rays of the sun refresh your sense of growing old, nor the scratched
Tree-trunks and mossy foliage, only immaculate darkness and thunder."
She grabbed Sweetpea. "I'm taking the brat to the country."
"But you can't do that—he hasn't even finished his spinach,"
Urged the Sea Hag, looking fearfully around at the apartment.

But Olive was already out of earshot. Now the apartment
Succumbed to a strange new hush. "Actually it's quite pleasant
Here," thought the Sea Hag. "If this is all we need fear from spinach

Then I don't mind so much. Perhaps we could invite Alice the Goon over"—
     she scratched
One dug pensively—"but Wimpy is such a country
Bumpkin, always burping like that." Minute at first, the thunder

Soon filled the apartment. It was domestic thunder,
The color of spinach. Popeye chuckled and scratched
His balls: it sure was pleasant to spend a day in the country.

Definition of Blue

The rise of capitalism parallels the advance of romanticism
And the individual is dominant until the close of the nineteenth century.
In our own time, mass practices have sought to submerge the personality
By ignoring it, which has caused it instead to branch out in all directions
Far from the permanent tug that used to be its notion of "home."
These different impetuses are received from everywhere
And are as instantly snapped back, hitting through the cold atmosphere
In one steady, intense line.

There is no remedy for this "packaging" which has supplanted the old sensations.
Formerly there would have been architectural screens at the point where the
    action became most difficult
As a path trails off into shrubbery—confusing, forgotten, yet continuing to exist.
But today there is no point in looking to imaginative new methods
Since all of them are in constant use. The most that can be said for them further
Is that erosion produces a kind of dust or exaggerated pumice
Which fills space and transforms it, becoming a medium
In which it is possible to recognize oneself.

Each new diversion adds its accurate touch to the ensemble, and so
A portrait, smooth as glass, is built up out of multiple corrections
And it has no relation to the space or time in which it was lived.
Only its existence is a part of all being, and is therefore, I suppose, to be prized
Beyond chasms of night that fight us
By being hidden and present.

And yet it results in a downward motion, or rather a floating one
In which the blue surroundings drift slowly up and past you
To realize themselves some day, while, you, in this nether world that could not
    be better
Waken each morning to the exact value of what you did and said, which
    remains.

The One Thing That Can Save America

Is anything central?
Orchards flung out on the land,
Urban forests, rustic plantations, knee-high hills?
Are place names central?
Elm Grove, Adcock Corner, Story Book Farm?
As they concur with a rush at eye level
Beating themselves into eyes which have had enough
Thank you, no more thank you.
And they come on like scenery mingled with darkness
The damp plains, overgrown suburbs,
Places of known civic pride, of civil obscurity.

These are connected to my version of America
But the juice is elsewhere.
This morning as I walked out of your room
After breakfast crosshatched with
Backward and forward glances, backward into light,
Forward into unfamiliar light,
Was it our doing, and was it
The material, the lumber of life, or of lives
We were measuring, counting?
A mood soon to be forgotten
In crossed girders of light, cool downtown shadow
In this morning that has seized us again?

I know that I braid too much my own
Snapped-off perceptions of things as they come to me.
They are private and always will be.
Where then are the private turns of event
Destined to boom later like golden chimes
Released over a city from a highest tower?
The quirky things that happen to me, and I tell you,
And you instantly know what I mean?
What remote orchard reached by winding roads
Hides them? Where are these roots?

It is the lumps and trials
That tell us whether we shall be known
And whether our fate can be exemplary, like a star.
All the rest is waiting

For a letter that never arrives,
Day after day, the exasperation
Until finally you have ripped it open not knowing what it is,
The two envelope halves lying on a plate.
The message was wise, and seemingly
Dictated a long time ago.
Its truth is timeless, but its time has still
Not arrived, telling of danger, and the mostly limited
Steps that can be taken against danger
Now and in the future, in cool yards,
In quiet small houses in the country,
Our country, in fenced areas, in cool shady streets.

City Afternoon

A veil of haze protects this
Long-ago afternoon forgotten by everybody
In this photograph, most of them now
Sucked screaming through old age and death.

If one could seize America
Or at least a fine forgetfulness
That seeps into our outline
Defining our volumes with a stain
That is fleeting too

But commemorates
Because it does define, after all:
Gray garlands, that threesome
Waiting for the light to change,
Air lifting the hair of one
Upside down in the reflecting pool.

Self-Portrait in a Convex Mirror

As Parmigianino did it, the right hand
Bigger than the head, thrust at the viewer
And swerving easily away, as though to protect
What it advertises. A few leaded panes, old beams,
Fur, pleated muslin, a coral ring run together
In a movement supporting the face, which swims
Toward and away like the hand
Except that it is in repose. It is what is
Sequestered. Vasari says, "Francesco one day set himself
To take his own portrait, looking at himself for that purpose
In a convex mirror, such as is used by barbers . . .
He accordingly caused a ball of wood to be made
By a turner, and having divided it in half and
Brought it to the size of the mirror, he set himself
With great art to copy all that he saw in the glass,"
Chiefly his reflection, of which the portrait
Is the reflection once removed.
The glass chose to reflect only what he saw
Which was enough for his purpose: his image
Glazed, embalmed, projected at a 180-degree angle.
The time of day or the density of the light
Adhering to the face keeps it
Lively and intact in a recurring wave
Of arrival. The soul establishes itself.
But how far can it swim out through the eyes
And still return safely to its nest? The surface
Of the mirror being convex, the distance increases
Significantly; that is, enough to make the point
That the soul is a captive, treated humanely, kept
In suspension, unable to advance much farther
Than your look as it intercepts the picture.
Pope Clement and his court were "stupefied"
By it, according to Vasari, and promised a commission
That never materialized. The soul has to stay where it is,
Even though restless, hearing raindrops at the pane,
The sighing of autumn leaves thrashed by the wind,
Longing to be free, outside, but it must stay
Posing in this place. It must move
As little as possible. This is what the portrait says.
But there is in that gaze a combination

Of tenderness, amusement and regret, so powerful
In its restraint that one cannot look for long.
The secret is too plain. The pity of it smarts,
Makes hot tears spurt: that the soul is not a soul,
Has no secret, is small, and it fits
Its hollow perfectly: its room, our moment of attention.
That is the tune but there are no words.
The words are only speculation
(From the Latin *speculum*, mirror):
They seek and cannot find the meaning of the music.
We see only postures of the dream,
Riders of the motion that swings the face
Into view under evening skies, with no
False disarray as proof of authenticity.
But it is life englobed.
One would like to stick one's hand
Out of the globe, but its dimension,
What carries it, will not allow it.
No doubt it is this, not the reflex
To hide something, which makes the hand loom large
As it retreats slightly. There is no way
To build it flat like a section of wall:
It must join the segment of a circle,
Roving back to the body of which it seems
So unlikely a part, to fence in and shore up the face
On which the effort of this condition reads
Like a pinpoint of a smile, a spark
Or star one is not sure of having seen
As darkness resumes. A perverse light whose
Imperative of subtlety dooms in advance its
Conceit to light up: unimportant but meant.
Francesco, your hand is big enough
To wreck the sphere, and too big,
One would think, to weave delicate meshes
That only argue its further detention.
(Big, but not coarse, merely on another scale,
Like a dozing whale on the sea bottom
In relation to the tiny, self-important ship
On the surface.) But your eyes proclaim
That everything is surface. The surface is what's there
And nothing can exist except what's there.
There are no recesses in the room, only alcoves,
And the window doesn't matter much, or that

Sliver of window or mirror on the right, even
As a gauge of the weather, which in French is
Le temps, the word for time, and which
Follows a course wherein changes are merely
Features of the whole. The whole is stable within
Instability, a globe like ours, resting
On a pedestal of vacuum, a ping-pong ball
Secure on its jet of water.
And just as there are no words for the surface, that is,
No words to say what it really is, that it is not
Superficial but a visible core, then there is
No way out of the problem of pathos vs. experience.
You will stay on, restive, serene in
Your gesture which is neither embrace nor warning
But which holds something of both in pure
Affirmation that doesn't affirm anything.

The balloon pops, the attention
Turns dully away. Clouds
In the puddle stir up into sawtoothed fragments.
I think of the friends
Who came to see me, of what yesterday
Was like. A peculiar slant
Of memory that intrudes on the dreaming model
In the silence of the studio as he considers
Lifting the pencil to the self-portrait.
How many people came and stayed a certain time,
Uttered light or dark speech that became part of you
Like light behind windblown fog and sand,
Filtered and influenced by it, until no part
Remains that is surely you. Those voices in the dusk
Have told you all and still the tale goes on
In the form of memories deposited in irregular
Clumps of crystals. Whose curved hand controls,
Francesco, the turning seasons and the thoughts
That peel off and fly away at breathless speeds
Like the last stubborn leaves ripped
From wet branches? I see in this only the chaos
Of your round mirror which organizes everything
Around the polestar of your eyes which are empty,
Know nothing, dream but reveal nothing.
I feel the carousel starting slowly
And going faster and faster: desk, papers, books,

Photographs of friends, the window and the trees
Merging in one neutral band that surrounds
Me on all sides, everywhere I look.
And I cannot explain the action of leveling,
Why it should all boil down to one
Uniform substance, a magma of interiors.
My guide in these matters is your self,
Firm, oblique, accepting everything with the same
Wraith of a smile, and as time speeds up so that it is soon
Much later, I can know only the straight way out,
The distance between us. Long ago
The strewn evidence meant something,
The small accidents and pleasures
Of the day as it moved gracelessly on,
A housewife doing chores. Impossible now
To restore those properties in the silver blur that is
The record of what you accomplished by sitting down
"With great art to copy all that you saw in the glass"
So as to perfect and rule out the extraneous
Forever. In the circle of your intentions certain spars
Remain that perpetuate the enchantment of self with self:
Eyebeams, muslin, coral. It doesn't matter
Because these are things as they are today
Before one's shadow ever grew
Out of the field into thoughts of tomorrow.

Tomorrow is easy, but today is uncharted,
Desolate, reluctant as any landscape
To yield what are laws of perspective
After all only to the painter's deep
Mistrust, a weak instrument though
Necessary. Of course some things
Are possible, it knows, but it doesn't know
Which ones. Some day we will try
To do as many things as are possible
And perhaps we shall succeed at a handful
Of them, but this will not have anything
To do with what is promised today, our
Landscape sweeping out from us to disappear
On the horizon. Today enough of a cover burnishes
To keep the supposition of promises together
In one piece of surface, letting one ramble
Back home from them so that these

Even stronger possibilities can remain
Whole without being tested. Actually
The skin of the bubble-chamber's as tough as
Reptile eggs; everything gets "programmed" there
In due course: more keeps getting included
Without adding to the sum, and just as one
Gets accustomed to a noise that
Kept one awake but now no longer does,
So the room contains this flow like an hourglass
Without varying in climate or quality
(Except perhaps to brighten bleakly and almost
Invisibly, in a focus of sharpening toward death—more
Of this later). What should be the vacuum of a dream
Becomes continually replete as the source of dreams
Is being tapped so that this one dream
May wax, flourish like a cabbage rose,
Defying sumptuary laws, leaving us
To awake and try to begin living in what
Has now become a slum. Sydney Freedberg in his
Parmigianino says of it: "Realism in this portrait
No longer produces an objective truth, but a *bizarria. . . .*
However its distortion does not create
A feeling of disharmony. . . . The forms retain
A strong measure of ideal beauty," because
Fed by our dreams, so inconsequential until one day
We notice the hole they left. Now their importance
If not their meaning is plain. They were to nourish
A dream which includes them all, as they are
Finally reversed in the accumulating mirror.
They seemed strange because we couldn't actually see them.
And we realize this only at a point where they lapse
Like a wave breaking on a rock, giving up
Its shape in a gesture which expresses that shape.
The forms retain a strong measure of ideal beauty
As they forage in secret on our idea of distortion.
Why be unhappy with this arrangement, since
Dreams prolong us as they are absorbed?
Something like living occurs, a movement
Out of the dream into its codification.

As I start to forget it
It presents its stereotype again
But it is an unfamiliar stereotype, the face

Riding at anchor, issued from hazards, soon
To accost others, "rather angel than man" (Vasari).
Perhaps an angel looks like everything
We have forgotten, I mean forgotten
Things that don't seem familiar when
We meet them again, lost beyond telling
Which were ours once. This would be the point
Of invading the privacy of this man who
"Dabbled in alchemy, but whose wish
Here was not to examine the subtleties of art
In a detached, scientific spirit: he wished through them
To impart the sense of novelty and amazement to the spectator"
(Freedberg). Later portraits such as the Uffizi
"Gentleman," the Borghese "Young Prelate" and
The Naples "Antea" issue from Mannerist
Tensions, but here, as Freedberg points out,
The surprise, the tension are in the concept
Rather than its realization.
The consonance of the High Renaissance
Is present, though distorted by the mirror.
What is novel is the extreme care in rendering
The velleities of the rounded reflecting surface
(It is the first mirror portrait),
So that you could be fooled for a moment
Before you realize the reflection
Isn't yours. You feel then like one of those
Hoffmann characters who have been deprived
Of a reflection, except that the whole of me
Is seen to be supplanted by the strict
Otherness of the painter in his
Other room. We have surprised him
At work, but no, he has surprised us
As he works. The picture is almost finished,
The surprise almost over, as when one looks out,
Startled by a snowfall which even now is
Ending in specks and sparkles of snow.
It happened while you were inside, asleep,
And there is no reason why you should have
Been awake for it, except that the day
Is ending and it will be hard for you
To get to sleep tonight, at least until late.

The shadow of the city injects its own
Urgency: Rome where Francesco
Was at work during the Sack: his inventions
Amazed the soldiers who burst in on him;
They decided to spare his life, but he left soon after;
Vienna where the painting is today, where
I saw it with Pierre in the summer of 1959; New York
Where I am now, which is a logarithm
Of other cities. Our landscape
Is alive with filiations, shuttlings;
Business is carried on by look, gesture,
Hearsay. It is another life to the city,
The backing of the looking glass of the
Unidentified but precisely sketched studio. It wants
To siphon off the life of the studio, deflate
Its mapped space to enactments, island it.
That operation has been temporarily stalled
But something new is on the way, a new preciosity
In the wind. Can you stand it,
Francesco? Are you strong enough for it?
This wind brings what it knows not, is
Self-propelled, blind, has no notion
Of itself. It is inertia that once
Acknowledged saps all activity, secret or public:
Whispers of the word that can't be understood
But can be felt, a chill, a blight
Moving outward along the capes and peninsulas
Of your nervures and so to the archipelagoes
And to the bathed, aired secrecy of the open sea.
This is its negative side. Its positive side is
Making you notice life and the stresses
That only seemed to go away, but now,
As this new mode questions, are seen to be
Hastening out of style. If they are to become classics
They must decide which side they are on.
Their reticence has undermined
The urban scenery, made its ambiguities
Look willful and tired, the games of an old man.
What we need now is this unlikely
Challenger pounding on the gates of an amazed
Castle. Your argument, Francesco,
Had begun to grow stale as no answer
Or answers were forthcoming. If it dissolves now

Into dust, that only means its time had come
Some time ago, but look now, and listen:
It may be that another life is stocked there
In recesses no one knew of; that it,
Not we, are the change; that we are in fact it
If we could get back to it, relive some of the way
It looked, turn our faces to the globe as it sets
And still be coming out all right:
Nerves normal, breath normal. Since it is a metaphor
Made to include us, we are a part of it and
Can live in it as in fact we have done,
Only leaving our minds bare for questioning
We now see will not take place at random
But in an orderly way that means to menace
Nobody—the normal way things are done,
Like the concentric growing up of days
Around a life: correctly, if you think about it.

A breeze like the turning of a page
Brings back your face: the moment
Takes such a big bite out of the haze
Of pleasant intuition it comes after.
The locking into place is "death itself,"
As Berg said of a phrase in Mahler's Ninth;
Or, to quote Imogen in *Cymbeline*, "There cannot
Be a pinch in death more sharp than this," for,
Though only exercise or tactic, it carries
The momentum of a conviction that had been building.
Mere forgetfulness cannot remove it
Nor wishing bring it back, as long as it remains
The white precipitate of its dream
In the climate of sighs flung across our world,
A cloth over a birdcage. But it is certain that
What is beautiful seems so only in relation to a specific
Life, experienced or not, channeled into some form
Steeped in the nostalgia of a collective past.
The light sinks today with an enthusiasm
I have known elsewhere, and known why
It seemed meaningful, that others felt this way
Years ago. I go on consulting
This mirror that is no longer mine
For as much brisk vacancy as is to be
My portion this time. And the vase is always full

Because there is only just so much room
And it accommodates everything. The sample
One sees is not to be taken as
Merely that, but as everything as it
May be imagined outside time—not as a gesture
But as all, in the refined, assimilable state.
But what is this universe the porch of
As it veers in and out, back and forth,
Refusing to surround us and still the only
Thing we can see? Love once
Tipped the scales but now is shadowed, invisible,
Though mysteriously present, around somewhere.
But we know it cannot be sandwiched
Between two adjacent moments, that its windings
Lead nowhere except to further tributaries
And that these empty themselves into a vague
Sense of something that can never be known
Even though it seems likely that each of us
Knows what it is and is capable of
Communicating it to the other. But the look
Some wear as a sign makes one want to
Push forward ignoring the apparent
Naïveté of the attempt, not caring
That no one is listening, since the light
Has been lit once and for all in their eyes
And is present, unimpaired, a permanent anomaly,
Awake and silent. On the surface of it
There seems no special reason why that light
Should be focused by love, or why
The city falling with its beautiful suburbs
Into space always less clear, less defined,
Should read as the support of its progress,
The easel upon which the drama unfolded
To its own satisfaction and to the end
Of our dreaming, as we had never imagined
It would end, in worn daylight with the painted
Promise showing through as a gage, a bond.
This nondescript, never-to-be defined daytime is
The secret of where it takes place
And we can no longer return to the various
Conflicting statements gathered, lapses of memory
Of the principal witnesses. All we know
Is that we are a little early, that

Today has that special, lapidary
Todayness that the sunlight reproduces
Faithfully in casting twig-shadows on blithe
Sidewalks. No previous day would have been like this.
I used to think they were all alike,
That the present always looked the same to everybody
But this confusion drains away as one
Is always cresting into one's present.
Yet the "poetic," straw-colored space
Of the long corridor that leads back to the painting,
Its darkening opposite—is this
Some figment of "art," not to be imagined
As real, let alone special? Hasn't it too its lair
In the present we are always escaping from
And falling back into, as the waterwheel of days
Pursues its uneventful, even serene course?
I think it is trying to say it is today
And we must get out of it even as the public
Is pushing through the museum now so as to
Be out by closing time. You can't live there.
The gray glaze of the past attacks all know-how:
Secrets of wash and finish that took a lifetime
To learn and are reduced to the status of
Black-and-white illustrations in a book where colorplates
Are rare. That is, all time
Reduces to no special time. No one
Alludes to the change; to do so might
Involve calling attention to oneself
Which would augment the dread of not getting out
Before having seen the whole collection
(Except for the sculptures in the basement:
They are where they belong).
Our time gets to be veiled, compromised
By the portrait's will to endure. It hints at
Our own, which we were hoping to keep hidden.
We don't need paintings or
Doggerel written by mature poets when
The explosion is so precise, so fine.
Is there any point even in acknowledging
The existence of all that? Does it
Exist? Certainly the leisure to
Indulge stately pastimes doesn't,
Any more. Today has no margins, the event arrives

Flush with its edges, is of the same substance,
Indistinguishable. "Play" is something else;
It exists, in a society specifically
Organized as a demonstration of itself.
There is no other way, and those assholes
Who would confuse everything with their mirror games
Which seem to multiply stakes and possibilities, or
At least confuse issues by means of an investing
Aura that would corrode the architecture
Of the whole in a haze of suppressed mockery,
Are beside the point. They are out of the game,
Which doesn't exist until they are out of it.
It seems like a very hostile universe
But as the principle of each individual thing is
Hostile to, exists at the expense of all the others
As philosophers have often pointed out, at least
This thing, the mute, undivided present,
Has the justification of logic, which
In this instance isn't a bad thing
Or wouldn't be, if the way of telling
Didn't somehow intrude, twisting the end result
Into a caricature of itself. This always
Happens, as in the game where
A whispered phrase passed around the room
Ends up as something completely different.
It is the principle that makes works of art so unlike
What the artist intended. Often he finds
He has omitted the thing he started out to say
In the first place. Seduced by flowers,
Explicit pleasures, he blames himself (though
Secretly satisfied with the result), imagining
He had a say in the matter and exercised
An option of which he was hardly conscious,
Unaware that necessity circumvents such resolutions
So as to create something new
For itself, that there is no other way,
That the history of creation proceeds according to
Stringent laws, and that things
Do get done in this way, but never the things
We set out to accomplish and wanted so desperately
To see come into being. Parmigianino
Must have realized this as he worked at his
Life-obstructing task. One is forced to read

The perfectly plausible accomplishment of a purpose
Into the smooth, perhaps even bland (but so
Enigmatic) finish. Is there anything
To be serious about beyond this otherness
That gets included in the most ordinary
Forms of daily activity, changing everything
Slightly and profoundly, and tearing the matter
Of creation, any creation, not just artistic creation
Out of our hands, to install it on some monstrous, near
Peak, too close to ignore, too far
For one to intervene? This otherness, this
"Not-being-us" is all there is to look at
In the mirror, though no one can say
How it came to be this way. A ship
Flying unknown colors has entered the harbor.
You are allowing extraneous matters
To break up your day, cloud the focus
Of the crystal ball. Its scene drifts away
Like vapor scattered on the wind. The fertile
Thought-associations that until now came
So easily, appear no more, or rarely. Their
Colorings are less intense, washed out
By autumn rains and winds, spoiled, muddied,
Given back to you because they are worthless.
Yet we are such creatures of habit that their
Implications are still around *en permanence*, confusing
Issues. To be serious only about sex
Is perhaps one way, but the sands are hissing
As they approach the beginning of the big slide
Into what happened. This past
Is now here: the painter's
Reflected face, in which we linger, receiving
Dreams and inspirations on an unassigned
Frequency, but the hues have turned metallic,
The curves and edges are not so rich. Each person
Has one big theory to explain the universe
But it doesn't tell the whole story
And in the end it is what is outside him
That matters, to him and especially to us
Who have been given no help whatever
In decoding our own man-size quotient and must rely
On second-hand knowledge. Yet I know
That no one else's taste is going to be
Any help, and might as well be ignored.

Once it seemed so perfect—gloss on the fine
Freckled skin, lips moistened as though about to part
Releasing speech, and the familiar look
Of clothes and furniture that one forgets.
This could have been our paradise: exotic
Refuge within an exhausted world, but that wasn't
In the cards, because it couldn't have been
The point. Aping naturalness may be the first step
Toward achieving an inner calm
But it is the first step only, and often
Remains a frozen gesture of welcome etched
On the air materializing behind it,
A convention. And we have really
No time for these, except to use them
For kindling. The sooner they are burnt up
The better for the roles we have to play.
Therefore I beseech you, withdraw that hand,
Offer it no longer as shield or greeting,
The shield of a greeting, Francesco:
There is room for one bullet in the chamber:
Our looking through the wrong end
Of the telescope as you fall back at a speed
Faster than that of light to flatten ultimately
Among the features of the room, an invitation
Never mailed, the "it was all a dream"
Syndrome, though the "all" tells tersely
Enough how it wasn't. Its existence
Was real, though troubled, and the ache
Of this waking dream can never drown out
The diagram still sketched on the wind,
Chosen, meant for me and materialized
In the disguising radiance of my room.
We have seen the city; it is the gibbous
Mirrored eye of an insect. All things happen
On its balcony and are resumed within,
But the action is the cold, syrupy flow
Of a pageant. One feels too confined,
Sifting the April sunlight for clues,
In the mere stillness of the ease of its
Parameter. The hand holds no chalk
And each part of the whole falls off
And cannot know it knew, except
Here and there, in cold pockets
Of remembrance, whispers out of time.

Street Musicians

One died, and the soul was wrenched out
Of the other in life, who, walking the streets
Wrapped in an identity like a coat, sees on and on
The same corners, volumetrics, shadows
Under trees. Farther than anyone was ever
Called, through increasingly suburban airs
And ways, with autumn falling over everything:
The plush leaves the chattels in barrels
Of an obscure family being evicted
Into the way it was, and is. The other beached
Glimpses of what the other was up to:
Revelations at last. So they grew to hate and forget each other.

So I cradle this average violin that knows
Only forgotten showtunes, but argues
The possibility of free declamation anchored
To a dull refrain, the year turning over on itself
In November, with the spaces among the days
More literal, the meat more visible on the bone.
Our question of a place of origin hangs
Like smoke: how we picnicked in pine forests,
In coves with the water always seeping up, and left
Our trash, sperm and excrement everywhere, smeared
On the landscape, to make of us what we could.

Pyrography

Out here on Cottage Grove it matters. The galloping
Wind balks at its shadow. The carriages
Are drawn forward under a sky of fumed oak.
This is America calling:
The mirroring of state to state,
Of voice to voice on the wires,
The force of colloquial greetings like golden
Pollen sinking on the afternoon breeze.
In service stairs the sweet corruption thrives;
The page of dusk turns like a creaking revolving stage in Warren, Ohio.

If this is the way it is let's leave,
They agree, and soon the slow boxcar journey begins,
Gradually accelerating until the gyrating fans of suburbs
Enfolding the darkness of cities are remembered
Only as a recurring tic. And midway
We meet the disappointed, returning ones, without its
Being able to stop us in the headlong night
Toward the nothing of the coast. At Bolinas
The houses doze and seem to wonder why through the
Pacific haze, and the dreams alternately glow and grow dull.
Why be hanging on here? Like kites, circling,
Slipping on a ramp of air, but always circling?

But the variable cloudiness is pouring it on,
Flooding back to you like the meaning of a joke.
The land wasn't immediately appealing; we built it
Partly over with fake ruins, in the image of ourselves:
An arch that terminates in mid-keystone, a crumbling stone pier
For laundresses, an open-air theater, never completed
And only partially designed. How are we to inhabit
This space from which the fourth wall is invariably missing,
As in a stage-set or dollhouse, except by staying as we are,
In lost profile, facing the stars, with dozens of as yet
Unrealized projects, and a strict sense
Of time running out, of evening presenting
The tactfully folded-over bill? And we fit
Rather too easily into it, become transparent,
Almost ghosts. One day
The birds and animals in the pasture have absorbed
The color, the density of the surroundings,
The leaves are alive, and too heavy with life.

A long period of adjustment followed.
In the cities at the turn of the century they knew about it
But were careful not to let on as the iceman and the milkman
Disappeared down the block and the postman shouted
His daily rounds. The children under the trees knew it
But all the fathers returning home
On streetcars after a satisfying day at the office undid it:
The climate was still floral and all the wallpaper
In a million homes all over the land conspired to hide it.
One day we thought of painted furniture, of how
It just slightly changes everything in the room
And in the yard outside, and how, if we were going
To be able to write the history of our time, starting with today,
It would be necessary to model all these unimportant details
So as to be able to include them; otherwise the narrative
Would have that flat, sandpapered look the sky gets
Out in the middle west toward the end of summer,
The look of wanting to back out before the argument
Has been resolved, and at the same time to save appearances
So that tomorrow will be pure. Therefore, since we have to do our business
In spite of things, why not make it in spite of everything?
That way, maybe the feeble lakes and swamps
Of the back country will get plugged into the circuit
And not just the major events but the whole incredible
Mass of everything happening simultaneously and pairing off,
Channeling itself into history, will unroll
As carefully and as casually as a conversation in the next room,
And the purity of today will invest us like a breeze,
Only be hard, spare, ironical: something one can
Tip one's hat to and still get some use out of.

The parade is turning into our street.
My stars, the burnished uniforms and prismatic
Features of this instant belong here. The land
Is pulling away from the magic, glittering coastal towns
To an aforementioned rendezvous with August and December.
The hunch is it will always be this way,
The look, the way things first scared you
In the night light, and later turned out to be,
Yet still capable, all the same, of a narrow fidelity
To what you and they wanted to become:
No sighs like Russian music, only a vast unravelling
Out toward the junctions and to the darkness beyond
To these bare fields, built at today's expense.

Wet Casements

*When Eduard Raban, coming along the passage, walked into the open
doorway, he saw that it was raining. It was not raining much.*
                    Kafka, *Wedding Preparations in the Country*

The concept is interesting: to see, as though reflected
In streaming windowpanes, the look of others through
Their own eyes. A digest of their correct impressions of
Their self-analytical attitudes overlaid by your
Ghostly transparent face. You in falbalas
Of some distant but not too distant era, the cosmetics,
The shoes perfectly pointed, drifting (how long you
Have been drifting; how long I have too for that matter)
Like a bottle-imp toward a surface which can never be approached,
Never pierced through into the timeless energy of a present
Which would have its own opinions on these matters,
Are an epistemological snapshot of the processes
That first mentioned your name at some crowded cocktail
Party long ago, and someone (not the person addressed)
Overheard it and carried that name around in his wallet
For years as the wallet crumbled and bills slid in
And out of it. I want that information very much today,

Can't have it, and this makes me angry.
I shall use my anger to build a bridge like that
Of Avignon, on which people may dance for the feeling
Of dancing on a bridge. I shall at last see my complete face
Reflected not in the water but in the worn stone floor of my bridge.

I shall keep to myself.
I shall not repeat others' comments about me.

Daffy Duck in Hollywood

Something strange is creeping across me.
La Celestina has only to warble the first few bars
Of "I Thought about You" or something mellow from
Amadigi di Gaula for everything—a mint-condition can
Of Rumford's Baking Powder, a celluloid earring, Speedy
Gonzales, the latest from Helen Topping Miller's fertile
Escritoire, a sheaf of suggestive pix on greige, deckle-edged
Stock—to come clattering through the rainbow trellis
Where Pistachio Avenue rams the 2300 block of Highland
Fling Terrace. He promised he'd get me out of this one,
That mean old cartoonist, but just look what he's
Done to me now! I scarce dare approach me mug's attenuated
Reflection in yon hubcap, so jaundiced, so *déconfit*
Are its lineaments—fun, no doubt, for some quack phrenologist's
Fern-clogged waiting room, but hardly what you'd call
Companionable. But everything is getting choked to the point of
Silence. Just now a magnetic storm hung in the swatch of sky
Over the Fudds' garage, reducing it—drastically—
To the aura of a plumbago-blue log cabin on
A Gadsden Purchase commemorative cover. Suddenly all is
Loathing. I don't want to go back inside any more. You meet
Enough vague people on this emerald traffic-island—no,
Not people, comings and goings, more: mutterings, splatterings,
The bizarrely but effectively equipped infantries of happy-go-nutty
Vegetal jacqueries, plumed, pointed at the little
White cardboard castle over the mill run. "Up
The lazy river, how happy we could be?"
How will it end? That geranium glow
Over Anaheim's had the riot act read to it by the
Etna-size firecracker that exploded last minute into
A *carte du Tendre* in whose lower right-hand corner
(Hard by the jock-itch sand-trap that skirts
The asparagus-patch of algolagnic *nuits blanches*) Amadis
Is cozening the Princesse de Clèves into a midnight micturition spree
On the Tamigi with the Wallets (Walt, Blossom, and little
Skeezix) on a lamé barge "borrowed" from Ollie
Of the Movies' dread mistress of the robes. Wait!
I have an announcement! This wide, tepidly meandering,
Civilized Lethe (one can barely make out the maypoles
And *châlets de nécessité* on its sedgy shore) leads to Tophet, that

Landfill-haunted, not-so-residential resort from which
Some travellers return! This whole moment is the groin
Of a borborygmic giant who even now
Is rolling over on us in his sleep. Farewell bocages,
Tanneries, water-meadows. The allegory comes unsnarled
Too soon; a shower of pecky acajou harpoons is
About all there is to be noted between tornadoes. I have
Only my intermittent life in your thoughts to live
Which is like thinking in another language. Everything
Depends on whether somebody reminds you of me.
That this is a fabulation, and that those "other times"
Are in fact the silences of the soul, picked out in
Diamonds on stygian velvet, matters less than it should.
Prodigies of timing may be arranged to convince them
We live in one dimension, they in ours. While I
Abroad through all the coasts of dark destruction seek
Deliverance for us all, think in that language: its
Grammar, though tortured, offers pavilions
At each new parting of the ways. Pastel
Ambulances scoop up the quick and hie them to hospitals.
"It's all bits and pieces, spangles, patches, really; nothing
Stands alone. What happened to creative evolution?"
Sighed Aglavaine. Then to her Sélysette: "If his
Achievement is only to end up less boring than the others,
What's keeping us here? Why not leave at once?
I have to stay here while they sit in there,
Laugh, drink, have fine time. In my day
One lay under the tough green leaves,
Pretending not to notice how they bled into
The sky's aqua, the wafted-away no-color of regions supposed
Not to concern us. And so we too
Came where the others came: nights of physical endurance,
Or if, by day, our behavior was anarchically
Correct, at least by New Brutalism standards, all then
Grew taciturn by previous agreement. We were spirited
Away *en bateau*, under cover of fudge dark.
It's not the incomplete importunes, but the spookiness
Of the finished product. True, to ask less were folly, yet
If he is the result of himself, how much the better
For him we ought to be! And how little, finally,
We take this into account! Is the puckered garance satin
Of a case that once held a brace of dueling pistols our
Only acknowledging of that color? I like not this,

Methinks, yet this disappointing sequel to ourselves
Has been applauded in London and St. Petersburg. Somewhere
Ravens pray for us."
                        The storm finished brewing. And thus
She questioned all who came in at the great gate, but none
She found who ever heard of Amadis,
Nor of stern Aureng-Zebe, his first love. Some
There were to whom this mattered not a jot: since all
By definition is completeness (so
In utter darkness they reasoned), why not
Accept it as it pleases to reveal itself? As when
Low skyscrapers from lower-hanging clouds reveal
A turret there, an art-deco escarpment here, and last perhaps
The pattern that may carry the sense, but
Stays hidden in the mysteries of pagination.
Not what we see but how we see it matters; all's
Alike, the same, and we greet him who announces
The change as we would greet the change itself.
All life is but a figment; conversely, the tiny
Tome that slips from your hand is not perhaps the
Missing link in this invisible picnic whose leverage
Shrouds our sense of it. Therefore bivouac we
On this great, blond highway, unimpeded by
Veiled scruples, worn conundrums. Morning is
Impermanent. Grab sex things, swing up
Over the horizon like a boy
On a fishing expedition. No one really knows
Or cares whether this is the whole of which parts
Were vouchsafed—once—but to be ambling on's
The tradition more than the safekeeping of it. This mulch for
Play keeps them interested and busy while the big,
Vaguer stuff can decide what it wants—what maps, what
Model cities, how much waste space. Life, our
Life anyway, is between. We don't mind
Or notice any more that the sky *is* green, a parrot
One, but have our earnest where it chances on us,
Disingenuous, intrigued , inviting more,
Always invoking the echo, a summer's day.

As We Know

All that we see is penetrated by it—
The distant treetops with their steeple (so
Innocent), the stair, the windows' fixed flashing—
Pierced full of holes by the evil that is not evil,
The romance that is not mysterious, the life that is not life,
A present that is elsewhere.

And further in the small capitulations
Of the dance, you rub elbows with it,
Finger it. That day you did it
Was the day you had to stop, because the doing
Involved the whole fabric, there was no other way to appear.
You slid down on your knees
For those precious jewels of spring water
Planted on the moss, before they got soaked up
And you teetered on the edge of this
Calm street with its sidewalks, its traffic,

As though they are coming to get you.
But there was no one in the noon glare,
Only birds like secrets to find out about
And a home to get to, one of these days.

The light that was shadowed then
Was seen to be our lives,
Everything about us that love might wish to examine,
Then put away for a certain length of time, until
The whole is to be reviewed, and we turned
Toward each other, to each other.
The way we had come was all we could see
And it crept up on us, embarrassed
That there is so much to tell now, really now.

At North Farm

Somewhere someone is traveling furiously toward you,
At incredible speed, traveling day and night,
Through blizzards and desert heat, across torrents, through narrow passes.
But will he know where to find you,
Recognize you when he sees you,
Give you the thing he has for you?

Hardly anything grows here,
Yet the granaries are bursting with meal,
The sacks of meal piled to the rafters.
The streams run with sweetness, fattening fish;
Birds darken the sky. Is it enough
That the dish of milk is set out at night,
That we think of him sometimes,
Sometimes and always, with mixed feelings?

A Driftwood Altar

I'll tell you what it was like:
If you could afford it, you could probably have had it,
no questions asked. If it ran well, hugged the road well,
cupped your body like a loose-fitting suit, there was only
the down payment; the rest is future memories.
Of all those who came near him at this stage, only
a few can describe him with any certainty: a drifter
was the consensus, polite with old people,
indifferent to children, extremely interested in young adults,
but so far, why remember him? And few did,
that much is certain. I caught up with him
on a back porch in Culver City, exchanged the requisite
nod, shirt biting into the neck. How is it with you and some
who have no meaning, to whom nothing pertains,
yet the emptiness is always with you,
crowding out sadness, a drum
to which the pagan is alerted, glances are exchanged,
and someone, whom later no one can recall, slips out the side door?

In the bathroom there was considerable embarrassment.
One had taken off without notice, and in the sludge
that washes up on the beach are papers to be signed,
seals to be affixed. O why in this case bother a stranger, there are
enough of us to oversee the caring, the docketing; there is even
warmth on these chilly evenings of late winter, a no-season, remembering
how hot and sharp it was only a few seasons ago
when they wore their coats such-and-such a length
and cars drove by, even as they do now in certain
precincts where the roads are washed and small, trivet-shaped flowers
appear a moment and are gone, to appease the musk-god, most certainly,
and people spill out of lobbies and their greetings thicken like silt
in the runoff from a glacier and it is the standard attitudes
that are struck, there is no cry, no escape from them?
O certainly one of you must have known all this,
had it plotted for him ahead of time and said nothing: certainly
one of you runs down to the road with the news, or to get help, perhaps.

Then the idol winks and pirogues with their slanting
rows of oarsmen are seen departing backwards with undue haste.
It is time to think of spring and in pockets of not extreme despair

or under the threat of a ragged-looking but benevolent cloud, a thought
occurs: we weren't always like this, something seemed to intervene
about halfway here; at any rate a great deal of action
scrapes what we are doing into shape, for the time being. Though I am lost
I can see other points on the island, remains of picnics nearer
than one had thought, and closer still the one who comes
to resolve it all, provided you sign a document
absolving others from their eternal responsibility, swearing
that you like this light, these birds, this rattling credo
as familiar as a banging shutter, and above all, promising not
just to go about your business but to do the thing, see it drained, emptied,
a box in which four seasons will again fit
just as they did once before fire took the sky
and airplanes in their spotted plumage were seen to waver, and sink, drifting
on the wind's tune that gets in cracks here, the same
old bore, the thing already learned.

For it is indecent to last long:
one shot of you aghast in the mirror is quite enough; fog mounts
gnarled roots of the trees and one could still
stop it in time. There has to be no story, although it is
bedtime and the nursery animals strike expectant, sympathetic poses.
And then in a quiet but tense moment the crossed
identities are revealed, the rightful heir stands in the doorway.
True, it is only a picture, but someone framed and hung it;
it is apposite. And when too many moods coincide, when all windows
give on destruction, its curfew anchors us
in logic, not reprehensible anymore, not even exemplary,
though emblematic, as some other person talking in an old car would be.

The History of My Life

Once upon a time there were two brothers.
Then there was only one: myself.

I grew up fast, before learning to drive,
even. There was I: a stinking adult.

I thought of developing interests
someone might take an interest in. No soap.

I became very weepy for what had seemed
like the pleasant early years. As I aged

increasingly, I also grew more charitable
with regard to my thoughts and ideas,

thinking them at least as good as the next man's.
Then a great devouring cloud

came and loitered on the horizon, drinking
it up, for what seemed like months or years.

Kenneth Koch

KENNETH KOCH

Kenneth Koch was born in Cincinnati in 1925, and grew up in the city's Avondale district. He was something of a prodigy at high school, scoring the highest possible mark in his SAT (Scholastic Aptitude Test). He enrolled in the University of Cincinnati, hoping to become a meteorologist, but his studies were interrupted when, at the age of eighteen, he was drafted into the army. In 1945 he was dispatched to the Pacific as a rifleman in the 96th Infantry Division; while en route to Okinawa, however, he contracted hepatitis and was evacuated to a hospital in Guam. He spent the rest of the war as a clerk-typist in Saipan in the Philippines.

By the time he was discharged in 1946, Koch had decided to devote his life to poetry. He had already had three poems published in *Poetry* magazine, the most important outlet for poetry at the time. He was accepted by Harvard as a transfer student, and immediately joined the likes of Robert Bly and Donald Hall on the staff of the *Advocate*. It wasn't, though, until he met John Ashbery in 1947 that he found someone who shared his iconoclastic poetic ideals and dislike of current conventions. In his senior year Koch won Harvard's most prestigious poetry prize, the Garrison, for his 'Entr'acte for a Freak Show' – a dramatic monologue spoken by a bearded lady. On graduating in 1948 he moved to New York, where he lived in the same building as the painter Jane Freilicher, on Third Avenue at 16th Street, in an apartment only yards from the tracks of the El. One of his favourite recreations there was to don a rubber gorilla mask and gaze out of his window at passing trains.

Koch's early work is heavily influenced by his absorption in the work of European writers such as Apollinaire, René Char, Paul Éluard, Raymond Roussel, and Federico Garcia Lorca. He spent a year in Aix-en-Provence on a Fulbright fellowship, where he experimented with systematic deformations of language that somewhat resemble the peculiar compositional methods of Roussel, whose work Koch discovered in 1951. In 'Days and Nights' Koch reveals the kinds of word-game he liked to use to generate surreal conjunctions and dislo-cations: 'Sweet are the uses of adversity / Became Sweetheart cabooses of diversity / And Sweet art cow papooses at the university / And Sea bar Calpurnia flower havens' re-noosed knees.' His most exhaustive experiment in this vein is the long poem *When the Sun Tries to Go On*, written in 1953, but not published in book form until 1969. Koch also, however, developed a very distinctive style of narrative poetry that is vivacious, colloquial, and at times almost manic in its attention to detail. He is an adept at pastiche – see for instance his 'Three Variations on a Theme of William Carlos Williams'. Humour is an essential part of Koch's concept of poetry, and is achieved by a wide range of means that include literary spoofing, tireless repetition – he is as devoted to lists as Whitman – and the deployment of a faux-naif tone of self-consciously demented exuberance. In a poem such as 'One Train May Hide Another' he expands the poem's *donnée* into a surreal catalogue of possible concealments that might go on forever: 'one sister may hide another... one bath may hide another... one hitchhiker may hide another...'

As the opening poem in this selection, 'Fresh Air', illustrates, Koch was the New York School poet most ready to engage in polemic with the poetic establishment, and the one most determined to promote the work of himself and friends to a wider audience. As a Professor of English at Columbia University he exerted a powerful influence over successive generations of students and poets. He thrived on interaction and collaboration, and there is an insistently social dimension to much of his work. He was an ambassador for poetry in the widest sense. He published two primers on the teaching of poetry in schools (*Wishes, Lies and Dreams*, 1970) and *Rose, Where Did You Get That Red?*, 1973) and a guide to the teaching of poetry in a nursing home (*I Never Told Anybody*, 1977) that have revolutionised approaches to Creative Writing. He also published numerous plays, and a book of short stories.

Koch spent most of his adult life in New York City. He received many prizes for his work, including the Bollingen Prize in 1995, for his *Selected Poems* and *One Train*, and the Phi Beta Kappa Poetry Award in 2000 for *New Addresses*. He died of leukemia in 2002.

Fresh Air

1

At the Poem Society a black-haired man stands up to say
"You make me sick with all your talk about restraint and mature talent!
Haven't you ever looked out the window at a painting by Matisse,
Or did you always stay in hotels where there were too many spiders crawling
      on your visages?
Did you ever glance inside a bottle of sparkling pop,
Or see a citizen split in two by the lightning?
I am afraid you have never smiled at the hibernation
Of bear cubs except that you saw in it some deep relation
To human suffering and wishes, oh what a bunch of crackpots!"
The black-haired man sits down, and the others shoot arrows at him.
A blond man stands up and says,
"He is right! Why should we be organized to defend the kingdom
Of dullness? There are so many slimy people connected with poetry,
Too, and people who know nothing about it!
I am not recommending that poets like each other and organize to fight them,
But simply that lightning should strike them."
Then the assembled mediocrities shot arrows at the blond-haired man.
The chairman stood up on the platform, oh he was physically ugly!
He was small-limbed and -boned and thought he was quite seductive,
But he was bald with certain hideous black hairs,
And his voice had the sound of water leaving a vaseline bathtub,
And he said, "The subject for this evening's discussion is poetry
On the subject of love between swans." And everyone threw candy hearts
At the disgusting man, and they stuck to his bib and tucker,
And he danced up and down on the platform in terrific glee
And recited the poetry of his little friends—but the blond man stuck his head
Out of a cloud and recited poems about the east and thunder,
And the black-haired man moved through the stratosphere chanting
Poems of the relationships between terrific prehistoric charcoal whales,
And the slimy man with candy hearts sticking all over him
Wilted away like a cigarette paper on which the bumblebees have urinated,
And all the professors left the room to go back to their duty,
And all that were left in the room were five or six poets
And together they sang the new poem of the twentieth century
Which, though influenced by Mallarmé, Shelley, Byron, and Whitman,
Plus a million other poets, is still entirely original
And is so exciting that it cannot be here repeated.

You must go to the Poem Society and wait for it to happen.
Once you have heard this poem you will not love any other,
Once you have dreamed this dream you will be inconsolable,
Once you have loved this dream you will be as one dead,
Once you have visited the passages of this time's great art!

2

"Oh to be seventeen years old
Once again," sang the red-haired man, "and not know that poetry
Is ruled with the sceptre of the dumb, the deaf, and the creepy!"
And the shouting persons battered his immortal body with stones
And threw his primitive comedy into the sea
From which it sang forth poems irrevocably blue.

Who are the great poets of our time, and what are their names?
Yeats of the baleful influence, Auden of the baleful influence, Eliot of the
    baleful influence
(Is Eliot a great poet? no one knows), Hardy, Stevens, Williams (is Hardy of
    our time?),
Hopkins (is Hopkins of our time?), Rilke (is Rilke of our time?), Lorca (is Lorca
    of our time?), who is still of our time?
Mallarmé, Valéry, Apollinaire, Éluard, Reverdy, French poets are still of our time,
Pasternak and Mayakovsky, is Jouve of our time?

Where are young poets in America, they are trembling in publishing houses
    and universities,
Above all they are trembling in universities, they are bathing the library steps
    with their spit,
They are gargling out innocuous (to whom?) poems about maple trees and
    their children,
Sometimes they brave a subject like the Villa d'Este or a lighthouse in Rhode
    Island,
Oh what worms they are! They wish to perfect their form.

Yet could not these young men, put in another profession,
Succeed admirably, say at sailing a ship? I do not doubt it, Sir, and I wish we
    could try them.
(A plane flies over the ship holding a bomb but perhaps it will not drop the bomb,
The young poets from the universities are staring anxiously at the skies,
Oh they are remembering their days on the campus when they looked up to
    watch birds excrete,
They are remembering the days they spent making their elegant poems.)

Is there no voice to cry out from the wind and say what it is like to be the wind,
To be roughed up by the trees and to bring music from the scattered houses
And the stones, and to be in such intimate relationship with the sea
That you cannot understand it? Is there no one who feels like a pair of pants?

3

Summer in the trees! "It is time to strangle several bad poets."
The yellow hobbyhorse rocks to and fro, and from the chimney
Drops the Strangler! The white and pink roses are slightly agitated by the
    struggle,
But afterwards beside the dead "poet" they cuddle up comfortingly against
    their vase. They are safer now, no one will compare them to the sea.

Here on the railroad train, one more time, is the Strangler.
He is going to get that one there, who is on his way to a poetry reading.
Agh! Biff! A body falls to the moving floor.

In the football stadium I also see him,
He leaps through the frosty air at the maker of comparisons
Between football and life and silently, silently strangles him!

Here is the Strangler dressed in a cowboy suit
Leaping from his horse to annihilate the students of myth!

The Strangler's ear is alert for the names of Orpheus,
Cuchulain, Gawain, and Odysseus,
And for poems addressed to Jane Austen, F. Scott Fitzgerald,
To Ezra Pound, and to personages no longer living
Even in anyone's thoughts—O Strangler the Strangler!

He lies on his back in the waves of the Pacific Ocean.

4

Supposing that one walks out into the air
On a fresh spring day and has the misfortune
To encounter an article on modern poetry
In New World Writing, or has the misfortune
To see some examples of some of the poetry
Written by the men with their eyes on the myth

And the Missus and the midterms, in the *Hudson Review*,
Or, if one is abroad, in *Botteghe Oscure*,
Or indeed in *Encounter*, what is one to do
With the rest of one's day that lies blasted to ruins
All bluely about one, what is one to do?
Oh surely one cannot complain to the President,
Nor even to the deans of Columbia College,
Nor to T. S. Eliot, nor to Ezra Pound,
And supposing one writes to the Princess Caetani,
"Your poets are awful!" what good would it do?
And supposing one goes to the *Hudson Review*
With a package of matches and sets fire to the building?
One ends up in prison with trial subscriptions
To the *Partisan, Sewanee,* and *Kenyon Review*!

5

Sun out! perhaps there is a reason for the lack of poetry
In these ill-contented souls, perhaps they need air!

Blue air, fresh air, come in, I welcome you, you are an art student,
Take off your cap and gown and sit down on the chair.
Together we shall paint the poets—but no, air! perhaps you should go to them,
    quickly,
Give them a little inspiration, they need it, perhaps they are out of breath,
Give them a little inhuman company before they freeze the English language to
    death!
(And rust their typewriters a little, be sea air! be noxious! kill them, if you
    must, but stop their poetry!
I remember I saw you dancing on the surf on the Côte d'Azur,
And I stopped, taking my hat off, but you did not remember me,
Then afterwards you came to my room bearing a handful of orange flowers
And we were together all through the summer night!)

That we might go away together, it is so beautiful on the sea, there are a few
    white clouds in the sky!

But no, air! you must go . . . Ah, stay!

But she has departed and . . . Ugh! what poisonous fumes and clouds! what a
    suffocating atmosphere!
Cough! whose are these hideous faces I see, what is this rigor

Infecting the mind? where are the green Azores,
Fond memories of childhood, and the pleasant orange trolleys,
A girl's face, red-white, and her breasts and calves, blue eyes, brown eyes,
    green eyes, fahrenheit
Temperatures, dandelions, and trains, O blue?!
Wind, wind, what is happening? Wind! I can't see any bird but the gull and I
    feel it should symbolize . . .
Oh, pardon me, there's a swan, one two three swans, a great white swan,
    hahaha how pretty they are! Smack!
Oh! stop! help! yes, I see—disrespect for my superiors—forgive me, dear Zeus,
    nice Zeus, parabolic bird, O feathered excellence! white!
There is Achilles too, and there's Ulysses, I've always wanted to see them,
And there is Helen of Troy, I suppose she is Zeus too, she's so terribly pretty—
    hello, Zeus, my you are beautiful, Bang!
One more mistake and I get thrown out of the Modern Poetry Association,
    help! Why aren't there any adjectives around?
Oh there are, there's practically nothing else—look, here's *gray, utter, agonized,*
    total, phenomenal, gracile, invidious, sundered, and *fused,*
Elegant, absolute, pyramidal, and . . . Scream! but what can I describe with these
    words? States!
States symbolized and divided by two, complex states, magic states, states of
    consciousness governed by an aroused sincerity, cockadoodle doo!
Another bird! is it morning? Help! where am I? am I in the barnyard? Oink
    oink, scratch, moo! Splash!
My first lesson. "Look around you. What do you think and feel?" *Uhhh . . .*
    "Quickly!" *This Connecticut landscape would have pleased Vermeer.* Wham!
    A-Plus. "Congratulations!" I am promoted.
OOOhhhhh I wish I were dead, what a headache! My second lesson: "Rewrite
    your first lesson line six hundred times. Try to make it into a magnetic
    field." I can do it too. But my poor line! What a nightmare! Here comes a
    tremendous horse.
Trojan, I presume. No, it's my third lesson. "Look, look! Watch him, see what
    he's doing? That's what we want you to do. Of course it won't be the
    same as his at first, but . . ." I demur. Is there no other way to fertilize
    minds?
Bang! I give in . . . Already I see my name in two or three anthologies, a serving
    girl comes into the barn bringing me the anthologies,
She is very pretty and I smile at her a little sadly, perhaps it is my last smile!
    Perhaps she will hit me! But no, she smiles in return, and she takes my
    hand.

My hand, my hand! what is this strange thing I feel in my hand, on my arm, on
    my chest, my face—can it be . . . ? it is! AIR!

Air, air, you've come back! Did you have any success? "What do you think?" I
    don't know, air. You are so strong, air.
And she breaks my chains of straw, and we walk down the road, behind us the
    hideous fumes!
Soon we reach the seaside, she is a young art student who places her head on
    my shoulder,
I kiss her warm red lips, and here is the Strangler, reading the *Kenyon Review*!
    Good luck to you, Strangler!
Goodbye, Helen! goodbye, fumes! goodbye, abstracted dried-up boys!
    goodbye, dead trees! goodbye, skunks!
Goodbye, manure! goodbye, critical manicure! goodbye, you big fat men
    standing on the east coast as well as the west giving poems the test!
    farewell, Valéry's stern dictum!
Until tomorrow, then, scum floating on the surface of poetry! goodbye for a
    moment, refuse that happens to land in poetry's boundaries! adieu, stale
    eggs teaching imbeciles poetry to bolster up your egos! adios, boring
    anomalies of these same stale eggs!
Ah, but the scum is deep! Come, let me help you! and soon we pass into the
    clear blue water. Oh GOODBYE, castrati of poetry! farewell, stale pale
    skunky pentameters (the only honest English meter, gloop gloop!)! until
    tomorrow, horrors! oh, farewell!

Hello, sea! good morning, sea! hello, clarity and excitement, you great expanse
    of green—

O green, beneath which all of them shall drown!

You Were Wearing

You were wearing your Edgar Allan Poe printed cotton blouse.
In each divided up square of the blouse was a picture of Edgar Allan Poe.
Your hair was blonde and you were cute. You asked me, "Do most boys think
    that most girls are bad?"
I smelled the mould of your seaside resort hotel bedroom on your hair held in
    place by a John Greenleaf Whittier clip.
"No," I said, "it's girls who think that boys are bad." Then we read *Snowbound*
    together
And ran around in an attic, so that a little of the blue enamel was scraped off
    my George Washington, Father of His Country, shoes.

Mother was walking in the living room, her Strauss Waltzes comb in her hair.
We waited for a time and then joined her, only to be served tea in cups painted
    with pictures of Herman Melville
As well as with illustrations from his book *Moby Dick* and from his novella,
    Benito Cereno.
Father came in wearing his Dick Tracy necktie: "How about a drink, everyone?"
I said, "Let's go outside a while." Then we went onto the porch and sat on the
    Abraham Lincoln swing.
You sat on the eyes, mouth, and beard part, and I sat on the knees.
In the yard across the street we saw a snowman holding a garbage can lid
    smashed into a likeness of the mad English king, George the Third.

Variations on a Theme by William Carlos Williams

1

I chopped down the house that you had been saving to live in next summer.
I am sorry, but it was morning, and I had nothing to do
and its wooden beams were so inviting.

2

We laughed at the hollyhocks together
and then I sprayed them with lye.
Forgive me. I simply do not know what I am doing.

3

I gave away the money that you had been saving to live on for the next ten years.
The man who asked for it was shabby
and the firm March wind on the porch was so juicy and cold.

4

Last evening we went dancing and I broke your leg.
Forgive me. I was clumsy, and
I wanted you here in the wards, where I am the doctor!

The Circus

I remember when I wrote The Circus
I was living in Paris, or rather we were living in Paris
Janice, Frank was alive, the Whitney Museum
Was still on 8th Street, or was it still something else?
Fernand Léger lived in our building
Well it wasn't really our building it was the building we lived in
Next to a Grand Guignol troupe who made a lot of noise
So that one day I yelled through a hole in the wall
Of our apartment I don't know why there was a hole there
Shut up! And the voice came back to me saying something
I don't know what. Once I saw Léger walk out of the building
I think. Stanley Kunitz came to dinner. I wrote The Circus
In two tries, the first getting most of the first stanza;
That fall I also wrote an opera libretto called Louisa or Matilda.
Jean-Claude came to dinner. He said (about "cocktail sauce")
It should be good on something but not on these (oysters).
By that time I think I had already written The Circus.
Part of the inspiration came while walking to the post office one night
And I wrote a big segment of The Circus
When I came back, having been annoyed to have to go
I forget what I went there about
You were back in the apartment what a dump actually we liked it
I think with your hair and your writing and the pans
Moving strummingly about the kitchen and I wrote The Circus
It was a summer night no it was an autumn one summer when
I remember it but actually no autumn that black dusk toward the post office
And I wrote many other poems then but The Circus was the best
Maybe not by far the best there was also Geography
And the Airplane Betty poems (inspired by you) but The Circus was the best.

Sometimes I feel I actually am the person
Who did this, who wrote that, including that poem The Circus
But sometimes on the other hand I don't.
There are so many factors engaging our attention!
At every moment the happiness of others, the health of those we know and our
    own!
And the millions upon millions of people we don't know and their well-being
    to think about
So it seems strange I found time to write The Circus
And even spent two evenings on it, and that I have also the time

To remember that I did it, and remember you and me then, and write this
        poem about it.
At the beginning of The Circus
The Circus girls are rushing through the night
In the circus wagons and tulips and other flowers will be picked
A long time from now this poem wants to get off on its own
Someplace like a painting not held to a depiction of composing The Circus.

Noel Lee was in Paris then but usually out of it
In Germany or Denmark giving a concert
As part of an endless activity
Which was either his career or his happiness or a combination of both
Or neither I remember his dark eyes looking he was nervous
With me perhaps because of our days at Harvard.

It is understandable enough to be nervous with anybody!

How softly and easily one feels when alone
Love of one's friends when one is commanding the time and space syndrome
If that's the right word which I doubt but together how come one is so
        nervous?
One is not always but what was I then and what am I now attempting to create
If create is the right word
Out of this combination of experience and aloneness
And who are you telling me it is or is not a poem (not you)? Go back with me
        though
To those nights I was writing The Circus.
Do you like that poem? have you read it? It is in my book Thank You
Which Grove just reprinted. I wonder how long I am going to live
And what the rest will be like I mean the rest of my life.

John Cage said to me the other night How old are you? and I told him forty-six
(Since then I've become forty-seven) he said
Oh that's a great age I remember.
John Cage once told me he didn't charge much for his mushroom identification
        course (at the New School)
Because he didn't want to make a profit from nature.

He was ahead of his time I was behind my time we were both in time
Brilliant go to the head of the class and "time is a river"
It doesn't seem like a river to me it seems like an unformed plan
Days go by and still nothing is decided about
What to do until you know it never will be and then you say "time"

But you really don't care much about it any more
Time means something when you have the major part of yours ahead of you
As I did in Aix-en-Provence that was three years before I wrote The Circus
That year I wrote Bricks and The Great Atlantic Rainway
I felt time surround me like a blanket endless and soft
I could go to sleep endlessly and wake up and still be in it
But I treasured secretly the part of me that was individually changing
Like Noel Lee I was interested in my career
And still am but now it is like a town I don't want to leave
Not a tower I am climbing opposed by ferocious enemies.

I never mentioned my friends in my poems at the time I wrote The Circus
Although they meant almost more than anything to me
Of this now for some time I've felt an attenuation
So I'm mentioning them maybe this will bring them back to me
Not them perhaps but what I felt about them
John Ashbery Jane Freilicher Larry Rivers Frank O'Hara
Their names alone bring tears to my eyes
As seeing Polly did last night.

It is beautiful at any time but the paradox is leaving it
In order to feel it when you've come back the sun has declined
And the people are merrier or else they've gone home altogether
And you are left alone well you put up with that your sureness is like the sun
While you have it but when you don't its lack's a black and icy night. I came
      home
And wrote The Circus that night, Janice. I didn't come and speak to you
And put my arm around you and ask you if you'd like to take a walk
Or go to the Cirque Medrano though that's what I wrote poems about
And am writing about that now, and now I'm alone

And this is not as good a poem as The Circus
And I wonder if any good will come of either of them all the same.

Fate

In a room on West Tenth Street in June
Of nineteen fifty-one, Frank O'Hara and I
And Larry Rivers (I actually do not remember
If Larry was there, but he would be there
Later, some winter night, on the stairway
Sitting waiting, "a demented telephone"
As Frank said in an article about him but then
On the stairs unhappy in a youthful manner, much
Happened later), Frank, John Ashbery,
Jane Freilicher and I, and I
Had just come back from Europe for the first time.
I had a bottle of Irish whiskey I had
Bought in Shannon, where the plane stopped
And we drank it and I told
My friends about Europe, they'd never
Been there, how much I'd loved it, I
Was so happy to be there with them, and my
Europe, too, which I had, Greece, Italy, France,
Scandinavia, and England—imagine
Having all that the first time. The walls
Were white in that little apartment, so tiny
The rooms are so small but we all fitted into one
And talked, Frank so sure of his
Talent but didn't say it that way, I
Didn't know it till after he was
Dead just how sure he had been, and John
Unhappy and brilliant and silly and of them all my
First friend, we had met at Harvard they
Tended except Frank to pooh-pooh
What I said about Europe and even
Frank was more interested but ever polite
When sober I couldn't tell it but
Barely tended they tended to be much more
Interested in gossip such as
Who had been sleeping with whom and what
Was selling and going on whereat I
Was a little hurt but used to it my
Expectations from my friendships were
Absurd but that way I got so
Much out of them in fact it wasn't

Causal but the two ways at once I was
Never so happy with anyone
As I was with those friends
At that particular time on that day with
That bottle of Irish whiskey the time
Four in the afternoon or
Three in the afternoon or two or five
I don't know what and why do I think
That my being so happy is so urgent
And important? it seems some kind
Of evidence of the truth as if
I could go back and take it? or do
I just want to hold what
There is of it now? thinking says hold
Something now which is why
Despite me and liking me that
Afternoon who was sleeping with
Whom was best and
My happiness picking up
A glass Frank What was it like Kenny
Ah from my being vulnerable
Only sometimes I can see the vulnerable-
Ness in others I have ever known
Faults with them or on the telephone
The sexual adventures were different
Each person at work autobiography all
The time plowing forward if
There's no question of movement as there
Isn't no doubt of it may I not
I may find this moment minute
Extraordinary? I can do nothing
With it but write about it two
Hundred forty West
Tenth Street, Jane's apartment,
Nineteen fifty-one or fifty-two I
Can never remember yes it was
Later or much earlier
That Larry sat on the stairs
And John said Um hum and hum and hum I
Don't remember the words Frank said Un hun
Jane said An Han and Larry if he
Was there said Boobledyboop so always
Said Larry or almost and I said

Aix-en-Provence me new sense of
These that London Firenze Florence
Now Greece and un hun um hum an
Han boop Soon I was at Larry's
And he's proposing we take a
House in Eastham—what? for the
Summer where is that and
Already that afternoon was dissipated
Another begun many more of
Them but that was one
I remember I was in
A special position as if it
Were my birthday but
They were in fact as if my
Birthday or that is to say Who
Cares if he grows older if
He has friends like
These I mean who does not
Care? the celebration is the cause
Of the sorrow and not
The other way around. I also went
To Venice and to Vienna there were
Some people I drove there
With new sunshine Frank says
Let's go out Jane John Frank
And I (Larry was not there, I now
Remember) then mysteriously
Left

The Simplicity of the Unknown Past

Out the window, the cow out the window
The steel frame out the window, the rusted candlestand;
Out the window the horse, the handle-less pan,
Real things. Inside the window my heart
That only beats for you—a verse of Verlaine.
Inside the window of my heart is a style
And a showplace of onion-like construction.
Inside the window is a picture of a cat
And outside the window is the cat indeed
Jumping up now to the top of the
Roof of the garage; its paws help take it there.
Inside this window is a range
Of things which outside the window are like stars
Arranged but huge in fashion.
Outside the window is a car, is the rusted wheel of a bicycle.
Inside it are words and paints; outside, smooth hair
Of a rabbit, just barely seen. Inside the glass
Of this window is a notebook, with little marks,
They are words. Outside this window is a wall
With little parts—they are stones. Inside this window
Is the start, and outside is the beginning. A heart
Beats. The cat leaps. The room is light, the sun is almost blinding.
Inside this body is a woman, inside whom is a star
Of some kind or other, which is like a uterus; and
Outside the window a farm machine starts.

To Marina

So many convolutions and not enough simplicity!
When I had you to write to it
Was different. The quiet, dry Z
Leaped up to the front of the alphabet.
You sit, stilling your spoons
With one hand; you move them with the other.
Radio says, "God is a postmaster."
You said, Ziss is lawflee. And in the heat
Of writing to you I wrote simply. I thought
These are the best things I shall ever write
And have ever written. I thought of nothing but touching you.
Thought of seeing you and, in a separate thought, of looking at you
You were concentrated feeling and thought.
You were like the ocean
In which my poems were the swimming. I brought you
Earrings. You said, These are lawflee. We went
To some beach, where the sand was dirty. Just going in
To the bathing house with you drove me "out of my mind."

It is wise to be witty. The shirt collar's far away.
Men tramp up and down the city on this windy day.
I am feeling a-political as a shell
Brought off some fish. Twenty-one years
Ago I saw you and loved you still.
Still! It wasn't plenty
Of time. Read Anatole France. Bored, a little. Read
Tolstoy, replaced and overcome. You read Stendhal.
I told you to. Where was replacement
Then? I don't know. He shushed us back into ourselves.
I used to understand
The highest excitement. Someone died
And you were distant. I went away
And made you distant. Where are you now? I see the chair
And hang onto it for sustenance. Good God how you kissed me
And I held you. You screamed
And I wasn't bothered by anything. Was nearest you.
And you were so realistic
Preferring the Soviet Bookstore
To my literary dreams.
"You don't like war," you said

After reading a poem
In which I'd simply said I hated war
In a whole list of things. To you
It seemed a position, to me
It was all a flux, especially then.
I was in an
Unexpected situation.
Let's take a walk
I wrote. And I love you as a sheriff
Searches for a walnut. And And so unless
I'm going to see your face
Bien soon, and you said
You must take me away, and
Oh Kenneth
You like everything
To be pleasant. I was burning
Like an arch
Made out of trees.

I'm not sure we ever actually took a walk.
We were so damned nervous. I was heading somewhere. And you had to be
At an appointment, or else be found out! Illicit love!
It's not a thing to think of. Nor is it when it's licit!
It is too much! And it wasn't enough. The achievement
I thought I saw possible when I loved you
Was that really achievement? Were you my
Last chance to feel that I had lost my chance?
I grew faint at your voice on the telephone
Electricity and all colors were mine, and the tops of hills
And everything that breathes. That was a feeling. Certain
Artistic careers had not even started. And I
Could have surpassed them. I could have I think put the
Whole world under our feet. You were in the restaurant. It
Was Chinese. We have walked three blocks. Or four blocks. It is New York
In nineteen fifty-three. Nothing has as yet happened
That will ever happen and will mean as much to me. You smile, and turn your
      head.

What rocketing there was in my face and in my head
And bombing everywhere in my body
I loved you I knew suddenly
That nothing had meant anything like you
I must have hoped (crazily) that something would
As if thinking you were the person I had become.

My sleep is beginning to be begun. And the sheets were on the bed.
A clock rang a bird's song rattled into my typewriter.
I had been thinking about songs which were very abstract.
Language was the champion. The papers lay piled on my desk
It was really a table. Now, the telephone. Hello, what?
What is my life like now? Engaged, studying and looking around
The library, teaching—I took it rather easy
A little too easy—we went to the ballet
Then dark becomes the light (blinding) of the next eighty days.
Orchestra cup became As beautiful as an orchestra or a cup, and
Locked climbs becomes If we were locked, well not quite, rather
Oh penniless could I really die, and I understood everything
Which before was running this way and that in my head
I saw titles, volumes, and suns I felt the hot
Pressure of your hands in that restaurant
To which, along with glasses, plates, lamps, lusters,
Tablecloths, napkins, and all the other junk
You added my life for it was entirely in your hands then—
My life
Yours, My Sister Life of Pasternak's beautiful title
My life without a life, my life in a life, my life impure
And my life pure, life seen as an entity
One death and a variety of days
And only one life.

I wasn't ready
For you.

I understood nothing
Seemingly except my feelings
You were whirling
In your life
I was keeping
Everything in my head
An artist friend's apartment
Five flights up the
Lower East Side nineteen
Fifty-something I don't know
What we made love the first time I
Almost died I had never felt
That way it was like being stamped on in Hell
It was roses of Heaven
My friends seemed turned to me to empty shell

On the railroad train's red velvet back
You put your hand in mine and said
"I told him"
Or was it the time after that?
I said Why did you
Do that you said I thought
It was over. Why? Because you were so
Nervous of my being there it was something I thought

I read
Tolstoy. You said
I don't like the way it turns out (*Anna
Karenina*) I had just liked the strength
Of the feeling you thought
About the end. I wanted
To I don't know what never leave you
Five flights up the June
Street emptied of fans, cups, kites, cops, eats, nights, no
The night was there
And something like air I love you Marina
Eighty-five days
Four thousand three hundred and sixty-
Two minutes all poetry was changed
For me what did I do in exchange
I am selfish, afraid you are
Overwhelmingly parade, back, sunshine, dreams
Later thousands of dreams

You said
You make me feel nawble (noble). I said
Yes. I said
To nothingness, This is all poems. Another one said (later)
That is so American. You were Russian.
You thought of your feelings, one said, not of her,
Not of the real situation. But my feelings were a part,
They were the force of the real situation. Truer to say I thought
Not of the whole situation
For your husband was also a part
And your feelings about your child were a part
And all my other feelings were a part. We
Turned this way and that, up-
Stairs then down
Into the streets.

Did I die because I didn't stay with you?
Or what did I lose of my life? I lost
You. I put you
In everything I wrote.

I used that precious material I put it in forms
Also I wanted to break down the forms
Poetry was a real occupation
To hell with the norms, with what is already written
Twenty-nine in love finds pure expression
Twenty-nine years you my whole life's digression
Not taken and Oh Kenneth
Everything afterwards seemed nowhere near
What I could do then in several minutes—
I wrote,
"I want to look at you all day long
Because you are mine."

I am twenty-nine, pocket flap folded
And I am smiling I am looking out at a world that
I significantly re-created from inside
Out of contradictory actions and emotions. I look like a silly child that
Photograph that year—big glasses, unthought-of clothes,
A suit, slight mess in general, cropped hair. And someone liked me,
Loved me a lot, I think. And someone else had, you had, too. I was
Undrenched by the tears I'd shed later about this whole thing when
I'd telephone you I'd be all nerves, though in fact
All life was a factor and all my nerves were in my head. I feel
Peculiar. Or I feel nothing. I am thinking about this poem. I am thinking about
     your raincoat,
I am worried about the tactfulness,
About the truth of what I say.
I am thinking about my standards for my actions
About what they were
You raised my standards for harmony and for happiness so much
And, too, the sense of a center
Which did amazing things for my taste
But my taste for action? for honesty, for directness in behavior?
I believe I simply never felt that anything could go wrong
This was abject stupidity
I also was careless in how I drove then and in what I ate
And drank it was easier to feel that nothing could go wrong
I had those feelings. I

Did not those things. I was involved in such and such
A situation, artistically and socially. We never spent a night
Together it is the New York of
Aquamarine sunshine and the Loew's Theater's blazing swing of light
In the middle of the day

Let's take a walk
Into the world
Where if our shoes get white
With snow, is it snow, Marina,
Is it snow or light?
Let's take a walk

Every detail is everything in its place (Aristotle). Literature is a cup
And we are the malted. The time is a glass. A June bug comes
And a carpenter spits on a plane, the flowers ruffle ear rings.
I am so dumb-looking. And you are so beautiful.

Sitting in the Hudson Tube
Walking up the fusky street
Always waiting to see you
You the original creation of all my You, you the you
In every poem the hidden one whom I am talking to
Worked at Bamberger's once I went with you to Cerutti's
Bar—on Madison Avenue? I held your hand and you said
Kenneth you are playing with fire. I said
Something witty in reply.
It was the time of the McCarthy trial
Hot sunlight on lunches. You squirted
Red wine into my mouth.
My feelings were like a fire my words became very clear
My psyche or whatever it is that puts together motions and emotions
Was unprepared. There was a good part
And an alarmingly bad part which didn't correspond—
No letters! no seeming connection! your slim pale hand
It actually was, your blondness and your turning-around-to-me look.
        Good-bye Kenneth.

No, Marina, don't go
And what had been before would come after
Not to be mysterious we'd be together make love again
It was the wildest thing I've done
I can hardly remember it

It has gotten by now
So mixed up with losing you
The two almost seem in some way the same. You
Wore something soft—angora? cashmere?
I remember that it was black. You turned around
And on such a spring day which went on and on and on
I actually think I felt that I could keep
The strongest of all feelings contained inside me
Producing endless emotional designs.

With the incomparable feeling of rising and of being like a banner
Twenty seconds worth twenty-five years
With feeling noble extremely mobile and very free
With Taking a Walk With You, West Wind, In Love With You, and Yellow Roses
With pleasure I felt my leg muscles and my brain couldn't hold
With the Empire State Building the restaurant your wrist bones with
        Greenwich Avenue
In nineteen fifty-one with heat humidity a dog pissing with neon
With the feeling that at last
My body had something to do and so did my mind

You sit
At the window. You call
Me, across Paris,
Amsterdam, New
York. Kenneth!
My Soviet
Girlhood. My
Spring, summer
And fall. Do you
Know you have
Missed some of them?
Almost all. I am
Waiting and I
Am fading I
Am fainting I'm
In a degrading state
Of inactivity. A ball
Rolls in the gutter. I have
Two hands to
Stop it. I am
A flower I pick
The vendor his

Clothes getting up
Too early and
What is it makes this rose
Into what is more fragrant than what is not?

I am stunned I am feeling tortured
By "A man of words and not a man of deeds"

I was waiting in a taxicab
It was white letters in white paints it was you
Spring comes, summer, then fall
And winter. We really have missed
All of that, whatever else there was
In those years so sanded by our absence.
I never saw you for as long as half a day.

You were crying outside the bus station
And I was crying—
I knew that this really was my life—
I kept thinking of how we were crying
Later, when I was speaking, driving, walking,
Looking at doorways and colors, mysterious entrances
Sometimes I'd be pierced as by a needle
Sometimes be feverish as from a word
Books closed and I'd think
I can't read this book, I threw away my life
These held on to their lives. I was
Excited by praise from anyone, startled by criticism, always hating it
Traveling around Europe and being excited
It was all in reference to you
And feeling I was not gradually forgetting
What your temples and cheekbones looked like
And always with this secret.

Later I thought
That what I had done was reasonable
It may have been reasonable
I also thought that I saw what had appealed to me
So much about you, the way you responded
To everything your excitement about
Me, I had never seen that. And the fact
That you were Russian, very mysterious, all that I didn't know
About you—and you didn't know

Me, for I was as strange to you as you were to me.
You were like my first trip to France you had
Made no assumptions. I could be
Clearly and passionately and
Nobly (as you'd said) who I was—at the outer limits of my life
Of my life as my life could be
Ideally. But what about the dark part all this lifted
Me out of? Would my bad moods, my uncertainties, my
Distrust of people I was close to, the
Twisty parts of my ambition, my
Envy, all have gone away? And if
They hadn't gone, what? For didn't I need
All the strength you made me feel I had, to deal
With the difficulties of really having you?
Where could we have been? But I saw so many new possibilities
That it made me rather hate reality
Or I think perhaps I already did
I didn't care about the consequences
Because they weren't "poetic" weren't "ideal"
And oh well you said we walk along
Your white dress your blue dress your green
Blouse with sleeves then one without
Sleeves and we are speaking
Of things but not of very much because underneath it
I am raving I am boiling I am afraid
You ask me Kenneth what are you thinking
If I could say
It all then I thought if I could say
Exactly everything and have it still be as beautiful
Billowing over, riding over both our doubts
Some kind of perfection and what did I actually
Say? Marina it's late. Marina
It's early. I love you. Or else, What's this street?
You were the perfection of my life
And I couldn't have you. That is, I didn't.
I couldn't think. I wrote, instead. I would have had
To think hard, to figure everything out
About how I could be with you,
Really, which I couldn't do
In those moments of permanence we had
As we walked along.

We walk through the park in the sun. It is the end.
You phone me. I send you a telegram. It
Is the end. I keep
Thinking about you, grieving about you. It is the end. I write
Poems about you, to you. They
Are no longer simple. No longer
Are you there to see every day or
Every other or every third or fourth warm day
And now it has been twenty-five years
But those feelings kept orchestrating I mean rehearsing
Rehearsing in me and tuning up
While I was doing a thousand other things, the band
Is ready, I am over fifty years old and there's no you—
And no me, either, not as I was then,
When it was the Renaissance
Filtered through my nerves and weakness
Of nineteen fifty-four or fifty-three,
When I had you to write to, when I could see you
And it could change.

Days and Nights

1. THE INVENTION OF POETRY

It came to me that all this time
There had been no real poetry and that it needed to be invented.
Some recommended discovering
What was already there. Others,
Taking a view from further up the hill (remnant
Of old poetry), said just go and start wherever you are.

It was not the kind of line
I wanted so I crossed it out
"Today I don't think I'm very inspired"—
What an existence! How hard to concentrate
On what is the best kind of existence!
What's sure is having only one existence
And its already having a shape.

Extase de mes vingt ans—
French girl with pure gold eyes
In which shine internal rhyme and new kinds of stanzas

When I said to F, Why do you write poems?
He said, Look at most of the poems
That have already been written!

All alone writing
And lacking self-confidence
And in another way filled with self-confidence
And in another way devoted to the brick wall
As a flower is when hummed on by a bee

I thought This is the one I am supposed to like best
The totally indifferent one
Who simply loves and identifies himself with something
Or someone and cares not what others think nor of time
The one who identifies himself with a wall.

I didn't think I was crazy
I thought Orpheus chasms trireme hunch coats melody
And then No that isn't good enough

I wrote poems on the edges of the thistles
Which my walking companions couldn't understand
But that's when I was a baby compared to now

"That is so much like you and your poetry."
This puts me in a self-congratulatory mood
Which I want to "feel out," so we sit together and talk
All through the winter afternoon.

I smoked
After writing five or ten lines
To enjoy what I had already written
And to not have to write any more

I stop smoking
Until after lunch
It is morning
It is spring
The day is breaking
Ten—eleven—noon
I am not smoking
I am asleep

Sense of what primitive man is, in cave and with primitive life
Comes over me one bright morning as I lie in bed
Whoosh! to the typewriter. Lunch! And I go down.

What have I lost?
The Coleridge joke, as W would say.

William Carlos Williams I wrote
As the end word of a sestina. And *grass*
Sleepy, hog snout, breath, and *dream.*
I never finished it.

I come down the hill—cloud
I like living on a hill—head
You are so lucky to be alive—jokes
It chimes at every moment—stung

So much of it was beyond me
The winding of the national highway
The fragments of glass in the convent wall

To say nothing of the habits of the bourgeoisie
And all those pleasures, the neat coat,
The bought wine, and the enabling of the pronouncements.

For Christ's sake you're missing the whole day
Cried someone and I said Shut up
I want to sleep and what he accomplished in the hours I slept
I do not know and what I accomplished in my sleep
Was absolutely nothing.

How much is in the poet and how much in the poem?
You can't get to the one but he gives you the other.
Is he holding back? No, but his experience is like a bubble.
When he gives it to you, it breaks. Those left-over soap dots are the work.

Oh you've done plenty I said when he was feeling despondent
Look at X and L and M. But they don't do anything, he replied.

At the window I could see
What never could be inside me
Since I was twelve: pure being
Without desire for the other, not even for the necktie or the dog.

2. THE STONES OF TIME

The bathtub is white and full of strips
And stripes of red and blue and green and white
Where the painter has taken a bath! Now comes the poet
Wrapped in a huge white towel, with his head full of imagery.

Try being really attentive to your life
Instead of to your writing for a change once in a while
Sometimes one day one hour one minute oh I've done that
What happened? I got married and was in a good mood.

We wrote so much that we thought it couldn't be any good
Till we read it over and then thought how amazing it was!

Athena gave Popeye a Butterfinger filled with stars
Is the kind of poetry Z and I used to stuff in jars

When we took a walk he was afraid
Of the dogs who came in parade
To sniffle at the feet
Of two of the greatest poets of the age.

The stars came out
And I was still writing
My God where's dinner
Here's dinner
My wife! I love you
Do you remember in Paris
When I was thinner
And the sun came through the shutters like a knife?

I said to so many people once, "I write poetry."
They said, "Oh, so you are a poet." Or they said,
"What kind of poetry do you write? modern poetry?
Or "My brother-in-law is a poet also."

Now if I say, "I am the poet Kenneth Koch," they say, "I think I've heard of you"
Or "I'm sorry but that doesn't ring a bell" or
"Would you please move out of the way? You're blocking my view
Of that enormous piece of meat that they are lowering into the Bay
Of Pigs." What? Or "What kind of poetry do you write?"

"Taste," I said to J and he said
"What else is there?" but he was looking around.

"All the same, she isn't made like that,"
Marguerite said, upon meeting Janice,
To her husband Eddie, and since
Janice was pregnant this had a clear meaning
Like the poetry of Robert Burns.

You must learn to write in form first, said the dumb poet.
After several years of that you can write in free verse.
But of course no verse is really "free," said the dumb poet.
Thank you, I said. It's been great talking to you!

Sweet are the uses of adversity
Became Sweetheart cabooses of diversity
And Sweet art cow papooses at the university
And Sea bar Calpurnia flower havens' re-noosed knees

A book came out, and then another book
Which was unlike the first,
Which was unlike the love
And the nightmares and the fisticuffs that inspired it
And the other poets, with their egos and their works,
Which I sometimes read reluctantly and sometimes with great delight
When I was writing so much myself
I wasn't afraid that what they wrote would bother me
And might even give me ideas.
I walked through the spring fountain of spring
Air fountain knowing finally that poetry was everything:
Sleep, silence, darkness, cool white air, and language.

3. The Secret

Flaming
They seem
To come, sometimes,
Flaming
Despite all the old
Familiar effects
And despite my knowing
That, well, really they're not flaming
And these flaming words
Are sometimes the best ones I write
And sometimes not.

The doctor told X don't write poetry
It will kill you, which is a very late example
Of the idea of the immortal killing the man
(Not since Hector or one of those people practically)
X either wrote or didn't I don't remember—
I was writing (what made me think of it)
And my heart beat so fast
I actually thought I would die.

Our idea is something we talked about, our idea
Our idea is to write poetry that is better than poetry
To be as good as or better than the best old poetry
To evade, avoid all the mistakes of bad modern poets
Our idea is to do something with language
That has never been done before

Obviously—otherwise it wouldn't be creation
We stick to it and now I am a little nostalgic
For our idea, we never speak of it any more, it's been
Absorbed into our work, and even our friendship
Is an old, rather fragile-looking thing.
Maybe poetry took the life out of both of them,
Idea and friendship.

I like the new stuff you're doing
She wrote and then she quoted some lines
And made some funny references to the poems
And he said have you forgotten how to write the other kind of poems
Or, rather, she said it I forget which
I was as inspired as I have ever been
Writing half-conscious and half-unconscious every day
After taking a walk or looking at the garden
Or making love to you (as we used to say)

Unconscious meant "grace"
It meant No matter who I am
I am greater than I am
And this is greater
And this, since I am merely the vessel of it,
May be the truth

Then I read Ariosto
I fell to my knees
And started looking for the pins
I had dropped when I decided to be unconscious
I wanted to fasten everything together
As he did and make an enormous poetry Rose
Which included everything
And which couldn't be composed by the "unconscious"
(At least not by the "unconscious" alone)

This rose became a bandanna, which became a house
Which became infused with all passion, which became a hideaway
Which became yes I would like to have dinner, which became hands
Which became lands, shores, beaches, natives on the stones
Staring and wild beasts in the trees, chasing the hats of
Lost hunters, and all this deserves a tone
That I try to give it by writing as fast as I can
And as steadily, pausing only to eat, sleep, and as we used to say, make love

And take long walks, where I would sometimes encounter a sheep
Which gave me rhyming material and often a flowering fruit tree,
Pear apple cherry blossom thing and see long paths winding
Up hills and then down to somewhere invisible again
Which I would imagine was a town, in which another scene of the poem could
    take place.

4. Out and In

City of eternal flowers
And A said Why not make it paternal flowers
And Z said Or sempiternal There were bananas
Lying on the closet shelf by the couch
Forty feet from where your miscarriage began
And we were talking about this nonsense
Which meant so much to us, meant so much to us at the time.

Ponte Vecchio going over the Arno
What an image you are this morning
In the eye of almighty God!
I am the old bridge he said she said
I forget if it was a boy or a girl
A sexless thing in my life
Like sidewalks couches and lunch

Walking around nervously then going in the house
The entire problem is to sit down
And start writing. Solved! Now the problem
Is to get up. Solved! Now the problem
Is to find something equally worthwhile to do. Solved!
Thank you for coming to see me. But
Thank you for living with me. And
Thank you for marrying me. While
Thank you for the arguments and the fights
And the deadly interpellations about the meanings of things!

Your blue eyes are filled with storms
To alter and mildly disarrange an image of someone's, he said it about the eyelid
But you are crying. I have a pain in my side.

The idea of Mallarmé
That

Well that it was so
Vital
Poetry, whatever it was
Is inspiring
Is I find even more inspiring
Than his more famous idea
Of absence
And his famous idea
Of an uncertain relationship of the words
In a line to make it memorably *fugace*.

Absence and I were often in my room
Composing. When I came out you and absence were wielding a broom
Which was a task I hadn't thought of in my absence
Finally absence took over
You, me, the broom, my writing, my typewriter,
Florence, the house, Katherine, everything.

Well, I don't know—those were great moments
Sometimes and terrible moments sometimes
And sometimes we went to the opera
And sometime later the automobile squeaked
There is no such thing as an automobile, there is only a Mercedes or a Ferrari
Or a Renault Deux Chevaux is that a Citroën
There is What do we care what kind of car but
Often in the sunshine we did. That's
When we were traveling I wasn't writing.

You've got to sit down and write. Solved!
But what I write isn't any good. Unsolved!
Try harder. Solved! No results. Unsolved!
Try taking a walk. Solved! An intelligent, pliable,
Luminous, spurting, quiet, delicate, amiable, slender line
Like someone who really loves me
For one second. What a life! (Solved!) Temporarily.

What do you think I should do
With all these old poems
That I am never going to even look at again
Or think about or revise—Throw them out!
But if I raise my hand to do this I feel like Abraham!
And no sheep's around there to prevent me.
So I take another look.

We asked the bad poet to come and dine
The bad poet said he didn't have time
The good poet came and acted stupid
He went to sleep on the couch
But grandiose inspiration had arrived for him with the wine
Such was the occasion.

Long afternoons, when I'm not too nervous
Or driven, I sit
And talk to the source of my happiness a little bit
Then Baby gets dressed but not in very much it's
Warm out and off we go
For twenty minutes or so and then come back.

Everyone in the neighboring houses
And in the neighboring orchards and fields
Is busily engaged in doing something
(So I imagine) as I sit here and write.

5. DAYS AND NIGHTS

A B C D F I J
L M N R Y and Z were the friends I had who wrote poetry
Now A B and C are dead, L N and Y have stopped writing
Z has gotten better than ever and I am in a heavy mood
Wondering how much life and how much writing there should be—
For me, have the two become mostly the same?
Mostly! Thank God only mostly! Last night with you
I felt by that shaken and uplifted
In a way that no writing could ever do.
The body after all is a mountain and words are a mist—
I love the mist. Heaven help me, I also love you.

When the life leaves the body life will still be in the words
But that will be a little and funny kind of life
Not including you on my lap
And looking at me then shading your beautiful eyes.

Do you want me to keep telling
You things about your
Poem or do you want me to stop? Oh
Tell me. What? I don't think

You should have that phrase "burn up" in the first line.
Why not? I don't know. It
Seems a little unlike the rest.

O wonderful silence of animals
It's among you that I best perhaps could write!
Yet one needs readers. Also other people to talk to
To be friends with and to love. To go about with: And
This takes time. And people make noise,
Talking, and playing the piano, and always running around.

Night falls on my desk. It's an unusual situation.
Usually I have stopped work by now. But this time I'm in the midst of a
     thrilling evasion,
Something I promised I wouldn't do—sneaking in a short poem
In the midst of my long one. Meanwhile you're patient, and the veal's cold.

Fresh spring evening breezes over the plates
We finish eating from and then go out.
Personal life is everything personal life is nothing
Sometimes—click—one just feels isolated from personal life
Of course it's not public life I'm comparing it to, that's nonsense vanity—
So what's personal life? the old mom-dad-replay joke or
Sex electricity's unlasting phenomenon? That's right. And on
This spring evening it seems sensational. Long may it be lasting!

It helps me to be writing it helps me to breathe
It helps me to say anything it gives me
I'm afraid more than I give it

I certainly have lost something
My writing makes me aware of it
It isn't life and it isn't youth
I'm still young enough and alive
It's what I wrote in my poems
That I've lost, the way Katherine would walk
As far as the tree line, and how the fruit tree blossoms
Would seem to poke their way into the window
Although they were a long way outside

Yes sex is a great thing I admire it
Sex is like poetry it makes you aware of hands feet arms and legs
And your beating heart

I have never been inspired by sex, always by love
And so we talk about "sex" while thinking a little about poetry

There are very few poems
Compared to all the thought
And the activity and the sleeping and the falling in love
And out of love and the friendships
And all the talk and the doubts and the excitement
And the reputations and the philosophies
And the opinions about everything and the sensitivity
And the being alone a lot and having to be with others
A lot and the going to bed a lot and getting up a lot and seeing
Things all the time in relation to poetry
And so on and thinking about oneself
In this somewhat peculiar way

Well, producing a lot, that's not what
Being a poet is about, said N.
But trying to do so is certainly one of the somethings
It is about, though the products I must say are most numinous—
Wisps of smoke! while novels and paintings clouds go belching over the way!

Poetry, however, lives forever.
Words—how strange. It must be that in language
There is less competition
Than there is in regular life, where there are always
Beautiful persons being born and growing to adulthood
And ready to love. If great poems were as easy to create as people—
I mean if the capacity to do so were as widespread—
Since there's nothing easy about going through a pregnancy—
I suppose we could just forget about immortality. Maybe we can!

Z said It isn't poetry
And R said It's the greatest thing I ever read
And Y said I'm sick. I want to get up
Out of bed. Then we can talk about poetry
And L said There is some wine
With lunch, if you want some
And N (the bad poet) said
Listen to this. And J said I'm tired and
M said Why don't you go to sleep. We laughed
And the afternoon-evening ended
At the house in bella Firenze.

One Train May Hide Another

(sign at a railroad crossing in Kenya)

In a poem, one line may hide another line,
As at a crossing, one train may hide another train.
That is, if you are waiting to cross
The tracks, wait to do it for one moment at
Least after the first train is gone. And so when you read
Wait until you have read the next line—
Then it is safe to go on reading.
In a family one sister may conceal another,
So, when you are courting, it's best to have them all in view
Otherwise in coming to find one you may love another.
One father or one brother may hide the man,
If you are a woman, whom you have been waiting to love.
So always standing in front of something the other
As words stand in front of objects, feelings, and ideas.
One wish may hide another. And one person's reputation may hide
The reputation of another. One dog may conceal another
On a lawn, so if you escape the first one you're not necessarily safe;
One lilac may hide another and then a lot of lilacs and on the Appia Antica one tomb
May hide a number of other tombs. In love, one reproach may hide another,
One small complaint may hide a great one.
One injustice may hide another—one colonial may hide another,
One blaring red uniform another, and another, a whole column. One bath may hide another bath
As when, after bathing, one walks out into the rain.
One idea may hide another: Life is simple
Hide Life is incredibly complex, as in the prose of Gertrude Stein
One sentence hides another and is another as well. And in the laboratory
One invention may hide another invention,
One evening may hide another, one shadow, a nest of shadows.
One dark red, or one blue, or one purple—this is a painting
By someone after Matisse. One waits at the tracks until they pass,
These hidden doubles or, sometimes, likenesses. One identical twin
May hide the other. And there may be even more in there! The obstetrician
Gazes at the Valley of the Var. We used to live there, my wife and I, but
One life hid another life. And now she is gone and I am here.
A vivacious mother hides a gawky daughter. The daughter hides
Her own vivacious daughter in turn. They are in

A railway station and the daughter is holding a bag
Bigger than her mother's bag and successfully hides it.
In offering to pick up the daughter's bag one finds oneself confronted by the
    mother's
And has to carry that one, too. So one hitchhiker
May deliberately hide another and one cup of coffee
Another, too, until one is over-excited. One love may hide another love or the
    same love
As when "I love you" suddenly rings false and one discovers
The better love lingering behind, as when "I'm full of doubts"
Hides "I'm certain about something and it is that"
And one dream may hide another as is well known, always, too. In the Garden
    of Eden
Adam and Eve may hide the real Adam and Eve.
Jerusalem may hide another Jerusalem.
When you come to something, stop to let it pass
So you can see what else is there. At home, no matter where,
Internal tracks pose dangers, too: one memory
Certainly hides another, that being what memory is all about,
The eternal reverse succession of contemplated entities. Reading *A Sentimental
    Journey* look around
When you have finished, for *Tristram Shandy*, to see
If it is standing there, it should be, stronger
And more profound and theretofore hidden as Santa Maria Maggiore
May be hidden by similar churches inside Rome. One sidewalk
May hide another, as when you're asleep there, and
One song hide another song; a pounding upstairs
Hide the beating of drums. One friend may hide another, you sit at the foot of a
    tree
With one and when you get up to leave there is another
Whom you'd have preferred to talk to all along. One teacher,
One doctor, one ecstasy, one illness, one woman, one man
May hide another. Pause to let the first one pass.
You think, Now it is safe to cross and you are hit by the next one. It can be
    important
To have waited at least a moment to see what was already there.

A Time Zone

On y loue des chambres en latin Cubicula locanda.
Je m'en souviens j'y ai passé trois jours et autant à Gouda

Apollinaire, Zone

A light from the ceiling is swinging outside on Forty-second Street traffic is
    zinging
Collaborating on The Construction of Boston is interesting
To construct the city of Boston Tinguely is putting up a big wall
Of gray sandstone bricks he is dressed in a French ball
Gown he puts the wall up during the performance
His costume is due to art and not to mental disturbance
Now the wall ten feet high is starting to tremble
People seated in the first rows run back for shelter
However the bricks stand firm Niki de St. Phalle dressed as Napoleon
Shoots at a Venus full of paint with a miniature (but real) cannon
Rauschenberg's rain machine's stuck it gives too much moisture
People look very happy to have gotten out of the theater
People ask that it be put on again but it can't be done
Tinguely with his hand bleeding says Boston can be constructed only once
And that is the end of that
Next day the Maidman Theatre stage is flat
I like the random absurdity of this performance
Done only once with nineteen-sixty-two-and-art romance
I meet Niki four years earlier in France in the spring
Five years before that I am with Janice and Katherine
In Greece two thousand years ago everything came crashing
We stand and try to imagine it from what is still standing
Years before this in Paris it's the boulevard Montparnasse
Larry Rivers is here he is living with a family that includes a dwarf
We are talking I have a "Fulbright" with us is Nell Blaine
I am pulled in one direction by Sweden in another by Spain
The idea of staying in Europe jolts me gives a convincing jerk
It's New York though where most of my friends are and the "new work"
Today with Frank O'Hara a lunch connection
The Museum of Modern Art is showing its Arp collection
Frank comes out of the doorway in his necktie and his coat
It is a day on which it would be good to vote
Autumn a crisp Republicanism is in the air tie and coat
Soon to be trounced by the Democrats personified as a slung-over-the-shoulder
    coat

Fascism in the form of a bank
Gives way to a shining restaurant that opens its doors with a clank
However before being taken into this odoriferous coffer
A little hard-as-a-hat poem to the day we offer
"Sky / woof woof! / harp"
This is repeated ten times
Each word is one line so the whole poem is thirty lines
It's a poem composed in a moment
On the sidewalk about fifteen blocks from the Alice in Wonderland Monument
Sky woof woof! harp is published in Semicolon
Later than this in this John Myers publication
O'Hara meanwhile is bending above his shirt
His mind being and putting mine on being on International Alert
There's no self-praise in his gossip
Which in fact isn't gossip but like an artistic air-trip
To all the greatest monuments of America and Europe
Relayed in a mild excited wide open-eyed smiling conversational style
Larry he says and Larry again after a while
He is crazy about Larry these two have a relationship
That is breaking the world's record for loquaciousness
I first meet Larry on Third Avenue
The El goes past and it throws into my apartment rust dust soot and what-
    have-you
Larry has a way of putting himself all out in front of himself
And stumbling through it and looking good while seemingly making fun of
    himself
This is my friend Larry Rivers says Jane Freilicher
She lives upstairs Larry is a sometime visitor
He is dedicated at this moment entirely to drawing
Abstract split-splot and flops and spots he finds a blur and boring
Give me a glass of pencil that hath been
Steeped a long time in Delacroix and Ingres nor does he neglect Rubens
He is drawing up a storm in his studio working hard
A little bit earlier he and Jane and others are bouleversés by Bonnard
Bonnard show at the Modern Museum
I meet these people too late to go and see them
I am of New York not a native
I'm from Cincinnati which is to this place's nominative like a remote dative
In 1948 from college I come here and finally settle
The city is hot and bright and noisy like a giant boiling kettle
My first connection to it aside from touristy is sexual
A girl met here or there at first nothing serious or contextual
That is earlier now I'm here to live on street subway and bus

I find people exciting unrecognizable and of unknown-to-me social class
Finally they start to come into focus
For a while it's like being at a play I may have the wrong tickets
On West Tenth Street now I am firmly settled in New York
I am a poet je suis poète but I'm not doing very much work
I'm in love with a beautiful girl named Robin
Her father has a hand-weaving factory he gives me a job winding bobbins
It is a one-floor loft in the garment district on Thirty-first Street
Pat Hoey visits someone next door on snow-white feet
Pat and I like to go to the ballet at the City Center
I get "Balanchined" as in a wine-press all Jacques d'Amboise has to do is enter
My poetry is somewhat stuck
It's taking me a little while to be able to write in New York
My painter friends help and what I am reading in the library
It is not the contemporary antics this happens later of John Ashbery
This shy and skinny poet comes down to visit me from "school"
When he and Jane Freilicher meet it's as if they'd both been thrown into a
    swimming pool
Afloat with ironies jokes sensitivities perceptions and sweet swift sophistications
Like the orchids of Xochimilco a tourist attraction for the nations
Jane is filled with excitement and one hundred percent ironic
This conversation is joy is speed is infinite gin and tonic
It is modernism in the lyrical laconic
Our relationship's platonic
With what intelligence linked to what beauty linked to what grassy gusty lurch
    across the canvas
Jane and her paintings I realize once again happiness
Huh? is possibly going to be available after long absence
Here today in a gray raincoat she appears
The style is laughter the subject may be a cause for tears
Larry has some of the qualities of a stand-up comic
He says of John Myers John Myers he always calls him that
John Myers never John John Myers says he isn't fat
Well doesn't have a fat EAR but look at his stomach
And oft at a party back his head he throws
And plays the piano singing a song he made up "My Nose"
His nose bothers and is thus conquered by Larry Rivers
He's doing a Bonnardesque painting it's so good it gives me "recognition" shivers
It's a room filled with women with somewhat beautiful fishlike graces
Mostly orangey-yellow they have sexy and sleepy looks on their faces the thick
Oil paint makes it look as if you'd stick
To it if you got next to it it also looks very spacious
Now Larry is sitting and smiling he is copying an Ingres

His hand is shaky his lines are as straight as coat hangers
Why don't you I say rather dumbly put something witty in your work
No Kenneth I can't he says prancing around like a funny Turk
Charcoal in one hand and making a little gesture with the other
One Sunday I go with him to the Bronx to visit his sister and his mother
Here I am with Larry's sister and his mother
Sitting in the kitchen above us is a motto
Joannie is blonde her brunette friend is warm and flushed as a risotto
I rather fancy her and Larry's mother fancies it stupid
To have invited this girl at the same time as me so interrupting the arrow of Cupid
Posing for Rivers his mother-in-law Berdie before a screen
Posing for her son-in-law this woman full and generous as the double issue of
     a magazine
The French *Vogue* for example or the *Ladies Home Journal*
Frank thinks her marvelous he finds the sublime in her diurnal
Larry is making a leafy tree out of metal
Here is his Jewish version of Courbet's painting of a funeral
Jane loves Matisse and is a fan of Baudelaire
In these paintings she is working on a secret of yellow blue and pink air
She and Larry make a big painting together
Larry with an unmeditated slash Jane with the perpetuity of a feather
That in a breeze is trying to pull itself together
I'm looking at the finished product it's rather de Kooningesque
Being de-Kooning-like some way is practically of being a New York painter the
     test
Here today though is not a de Kooning but one of Jane's it's luscious big and
     feminine
I am inspired by these painters
They make me want to paint myself on an amateur basis
Without losing my poetic status
Jane is demonstrating to me the pleasures of using charcoal
I am copying a Delacroix of a black woman called I think The Slave Girl
Erasing makes a lovely mess
It looks like depth and looks like distance
Ink at the opposite end of materials is deliberate and daring
No chance to erase it and oil pastels like wildflowers in a clearing
My Aesthetic I only paint for a few years is rather elementary
Get something that looks good looks real looks surprising looks from this century
I am sitting at a little table downstairs in the Third Avenue apartment
I like buying slabs of masonite and all kinds of equipment
At the Metropolitan on a big wall is a great big Rubens
Of a king and some nobles on horses bigger than cabins
I am walking through the European Collection

With Larry and Jane they're giving it a professional inspection
On drawing paper I'm doing some Seurat-like dotting
I like this even love it but I know it's going to come to nothing
It is invigorating to stand in this studio
John Ashbery comes to visit he is listening to Bob and Ray on our radio
It is a small old-fashioned console attacked by salt water
John finds them wheezingly amusing all over the house sounds his raucous
    laughter
He and I "go back" to Harvard College
Now he is sitting at his typewriter in Greenwich Village
He's just finished a poem and he's happy as after a good repast
He is certain this feeling won't last
John is predictably and pleasantly gloom-filled
I've just driven to New York from some place north of Bloomfield
I'm an hour and a half late
This enables John to finish his poem as I with mixed feelings find out
"The Picture of Little J.A. in a Prospect of Flowers"
He made good use of this couple of wasted hours
Dick gives Genevieve a swift punch in the pajamas
It's a vault over W. C. Williams and a bypass of Dylan Thomas
He is still sitting at his little portable
Being because of my poem-causing lateness exceptionally cordial
We are both fans of the old Mystery Plays
We also find each other mysterious in certain ways
This mystery becomes greater as more time passes
Then finally the mystery itself passes
We're at Harvard together
We walk along talking about poetry in the autumn weather
He is not writing much this year but he likes to collaborate
So do I we do a set of sestinas at a speedy rate
Six sestinas each about an animal with one concluding one called The Bestiary
There is also a three-page poem in which all the lines rhyme with the title The
    Cassowary
Next we do a poetic compendium called The New York Times
September Eighth Nineteen Fifty-One both with and without rhymes
Our poems are like tracks setting out
We have little idea where we're going or what it's about
I enjoy these compositional duets
Accompanied by drinking coffee and joking on Charles and Perry Streets
We tell each other names of writers in great secret
Secret but absolutely no one else cares so why keep it
We're writing a deliberately bad work called The Reconstruction of Colonial
    Williamsburg

In a feeble attempt to win a contest the style is the Kenyon Review absurd
Larry and Jane propose to me renting a house in East Hampton
We go sizzling out of the city with the rapidity of a flu symptom
No this is actually a year later my memory missed it
I now go to California to be a "teaching assistant"
This year goes by I meet the girl who is later my wife Janice
I love to kiss her and to talk to her very often it's talking about my friends
I also talk a lot about "Europe" and France
She's a little deflating and tells me that to be a great poet
I have to do something she tells me but I forget exactly what
I think have for all my poems some sort of system
I am shaken but still feel secure in my avant-garde wisdom
East Hampton glaringest of Hamptons Hampton of sea shine of de Kooning
    and of leaves
Frank's visiting we're composing a poem he tugs at his sleeves
It is a Nina we are composing it is a Nina Sestina
For Nina Castelli's birthday her adorable sixteenth one
This year this month this week in fact Frank writes "Hatred"
A stunning tour-de-poem on an unending roll of paper
It makes going on forever seem attractive
Writing in the manner of O'Hara means being extremely active
Twenty people are over then thirty now about forty
Zip Frank sits down in the midst and types out a poem it doesn't even seem arty
I try it out with little success
It's one of those things the originator can do best
"Hatred" is full of a thundering array of vocables
From it straight through to the Odes Frank's talent is implacable
Now here he is holding out to me a package
Of Picayunes he taps one on his kneebone-covering khakis
Finally we have a poem for Castelli's daughter
Moonlight dissolve next day we're visiting Anne and Fairfield Porter
Fairfield is in his studio a mighty man
Posing like fluttering then settling sea birds around him Jerry Katie Elizabeth
    and Anne
He has opinions that do not waver
On his canvases he creates a bright and wholesome fever
Flowers like little pockets of yellow and pink pigment
Are aspiring up to a tree or a wall or a house like a sunlight shipment
At a John Cage concert there is hardly a sound
It's the paradise of music lost and music found
I find it pure and great as if a great big flash of light were going off underground
Satie and Webern are hitting me in the head and so finally with the Cantos is
    Ezra Pound

Frank and I are writing very long poems
Long is really the operative word for these poems
His is called Second Avenue mine When the Sun Tries to Go On
I don't know where I got the title
I'm working on it every afternoon the words seem to me arriving like
    stampeding cattle
It's not at all clear but for the first time in my life the words seem completely
    accurate
If I write for three hours I allow myself a cigarette
I'm smoking it's a little too much I'm not sure I can get through it alone
Frank and I read each other segments of these long works daily on the phone
Janice finds it funny now that I've dropped this bunch of pages
That I can't get them back in the right order well I do but it's by stages
It is April I have a job at the Hunter College Library
I come down to the Cedar on a bus hoping to see O'Hara and Ashbery
Astonishingly on the bus I don't know why it's the only occasion
I write a poem Where Am I Kenneth? It's on some torn-out notebook pages
The Cedar and the Five Spot each is a usable place
A celebrated comment Interviewer What do you think of space? De Kooning
    Fuck space!
In any case Frank is there he says he likes Where Am I Kenneth?
I carry this news home pleasantly and the poem it mentions her to Janice
John's poem Europe is full of avant-garde ardor
I am thinking it's making an order out of a great disorder
I wonder at what stage in life does this get harder
The Cedar Bar one hardly thinks of it is what may be called a scene
However one closed to the public since no one goes there to be seen
It is a meeting place for the briefest romances
And here is Norman Bluhm at the bar saying Who cares about those nances?
And here he is shoving and here is de Kooning and there is a beer
Being flung at someone Arnold Weinstein or me through the smoke-talky
    atmosphere
Of this corner booth
Voici Guston and Mitchell and Smith and here on top of everything is Ruth
Kligman being bedazzling without stop
She writes a poem with the line At the bar you've got to be on top
Meanwhile tonight Boris Pasternak
Is awarded the Nobel Prize and is forced to give it back
Frank O'Hara is angry there seems both a flash and a blur in his eyes
Kenneth we've got to do something about Pasternak and the Nobel Prize
What? well we ought to let him know
That we support him Off flies a cable into the perpetual snow

Dear Boris Pasternak We completely support you and we also love your early
    work
Signed puzzlingly for him in the morning's glare if he ever receives it
    Frank O'Hara and Kenneth Koch
Staging George Washington Crossing the Delaware
Alex Katz comes up looking like a pear
He has some white plywood boards with him he says where
Shall I put this stuff and a big bare
Wall is the side of their emplacement No chair
For Alex painting and cutting And now they're there
The seven soldiers one cherry tree one Delaware crossing boat
Hey hey Ken cries Alex I've done it
I've made you a set for George Washington Crossing the Delaware
The British and American armies face each other on wooden feet
I write this play in our apartment on Commerce Street
I am working in the early afternoon and stay up late
Dawn is peeling oranges on top of the skyscrapers
On the stage a wall goes up and then it's taken down
And under the Mirabeau Bridge flows the Seine
Today Larry and Frank are putting together "Stones"
It's a series of lithographs
Larry puts down blotches violently they look like the grapes of wrath
Frank is smoking and looking his best ideas come in transit
I walk the nine blocks to the studio he says Come in
New York today is white dirty and loud like a snow-clogged engine
Huge men in undershirts scream at each other in trucks near Second Avenue
    and Tenth Street
De Kooning's landscapey woman is full of double-exposure perfections
Bob Goodnough is making some small flat red corrections
Jane is concentrating she's frowning she has a look of happy distress
She's painting her own portrait in a long-sleeved dark pink dress
I'm excited I'm writing at my typewriter it doesn't make too much sense

James Schuyler

JAMES SCHUYLER

James Schuyler was born in 1922 in Chicago, Illinois. His parents divorced in 1929, and he was brought up by his mother and step-father in Washington DC, Buffalo, and East Aurora. He entered Bethany College, a small university in West Virginia, in 1941, but seems to have done little work there. Instead he spent most of his time playing bridge. In 1943 he joined the navy, training to be a sonarman in Key West, at the same school O'Hara was to attend the following year. He was assigned to North Atlantic convoy duty on the USS *Glennon*. In 1944, however, Schuyler failed to return from a shore-leave in New York, and only reported himself to the authorities several weeks later. At the hearing that followed his homosexuality was revealed, and he was discharged.

After the war Schuyler travelled for two years (1947–9) in Europe, where he met Truman Capote, Tennessee Williams, and W.H. Auden. He spent the April of 1949 on Ischia, typing up the manuscript of Auden's *Nones*. 'Well, if this is poetry,' he later recalled thinking, 'I'm certainly never going to write any myself.' A couple of years after his return to New York he was introduced to Ashbery, O'Hara and Koch, all of whom encouraged his writing. He composed his first poems while recovering from the first of many mental breakdowns in Bloomingdale mental hospital in White Plains. On this occasion he was convinced he'd had a long conversation with the Virgin Mary, who'd informed him the Day of Judgement was at hand. He suffered a second collapse in 1961, and spent most of the 1970s in and out of various pyschiatric institutions. 'Wigging in, wigging out:' he drily observes in 'Trip', the first of 'The Payne Whitney Poems' (Payne Whitney is the psychiatric unit of New York Hospital); 'when I stop to think / the wires in my head / cross: kaboom.'

Much of Schuyler's poetry combines a delicate attention to detail with an unobtrusive but haunting lyricism. He was a great admirer of English diarists such as Dorothy Wordsworth, Parson Woodforde, and Gilbert White, and his shorter pieces often take the form of diary entries, while his long poems are like poetic journals in which he records over weeks or months the development of the weather, the landscape, and his own experiences, ideas, and fluctuating emotions.

and state of health. His oblique approach to the death of Frank O'Hara in 'Buried at Springs' is typical of his reticence and subtlety. Schuyler spent much tim staying with friends such as Fairfield Porter, Ron Padgett, and Kenward Elmslie, and his poems often function as tributes to their hospitality, as well as to aspects of the natural world he experienced on these extended vacations in Maine, Vermont, and Long Island. Many of Schuyler's most moving and effective poems were written during the 1970s, when his psychiatric problems were at their worst. Part of their power derives from a vein of grateful wonder that he has not yet succumbed to his illness: 'When I think / of that,' concludes 'Trip', 'that at / only fifty-one I, / Jim the Jerk, am / still alive and breathing / deeply, that I think / is a miracle.'

His narrowest escape occurred in April 1977, when he inadvertently caused a fire in his 20th Street rooming house by falling asleep with a lighted cigarette. Both breathing and pulse had stopped by the time he was rescued by the fire brigade. For the next couple of years he resided mainly in a series of mental hospitals, but on his release from Payne Whitney in 1979 he was able, thanks to a grant from the Frank O'Hara Foundation, to settle in the Chelsea Hotel on 23rd Street, where he enjoyed a period of much improved health. His *Selected Poems* was published to widespread acclaim in 1988. Despite his acute shyness, Schuyler finally agreed to give a poetry reading to celebrate the event. It was a great success, and over the next few years he gave several more. Schuyler died in St Vincent's Hospital on 12 April 1991, after suffering a stroke a week earlier in the Chelsea Hotel. His long residence there is commemorated in a plaque by the front entrance. His *Collected Poems* was published in 1993. Schuyler also wrote three wonderfully entertaining works of fiction that all testify to his love of the English novel of manners: *Alfred and Guinevere* (1958), *A Nest of Ninnies* (co-written with John Ashbery, 1969), and *What's for Dinner?* (1978).

February

A chimney, breathing a little smoke.
The sun, I can't see
making a bit of pink
I can't quite see in the blue.
The pink of five tulips
at five P.M. on the day before March first.
The green of the tulip stems and leaves
like something I can't remember,
finding a jack-in-the-pulpit
a long time ago and far away.
Why it was December then
and the sun was on the sea
by the temples we'd gone to see.
One green wave moved in the violet sea
like the UN building on big evenings,
green and wet
while the sky turns violet.
A few almond trees
had a few flowers, like a few snowflakes
out of the blue looking pink in the light.
A gray hush
in which the boxy trucks roll up Second Avenue
into the sky. They're just
going over the hill.
The green leaves of the tulips on my desk
like grass light on flesh,
and a green-copper steeple
and streaks of cloud beginning to glow.
I can't get over
how it all works in together
like a woman who just came to her window
and stands there filling it
jogging her baby in her arms.
She's so far off. Is it the light
that makes the baby pink?
I can see the little fists
and the rocking-horse motion of her breasts.
It's getting grayer and gold and chilly.
Two dog-size lions face each other
at the corners of a roof.

It's the yellow dust inside the tulips.
It's the shape of a tulip.
It's the water in the drinking glass the tulips are in.
It's a day like any other.

May 24th or so

Among white lilac trusses, green-gold spaces of sunlit grass.
The shade side of a clothes pole, dark innards of a light-violet shell.
Everything trembles
everything shakes
in the great sifter:
bud scales, pollen, all the Maytime trash
whose sprinkles are clocks that tell
the time of the dandelion take-over generation,
never quite coming to pass.
A man passes
in calendula-colored socks.
A robin passes

         zip

            thud

punctuating the typescript of today with a comma on the too-close
    cut grass.
Then erases it for a full stop in a lilac.
In Y's and V's and W's
an elm ascends
smoothly as an Otis Elevator.
Other trade-marks blur in the gone-over forsythia hedge.
A table and a chair, carved chunkily in the lawn,
are the colors of an oystershell as though beneath the sod were
    chalk not sand.
Why it seems awfully far
from the green hell of August
and the winter rictus,
dashed off, like the easiest thing

Buried at Springs

There is a hornet in the room
and one of us will have to go
out the window into the late
August mid-afternoon sun. I
won. There is a certain challenge
in being humane to hornets
but not much. A launch draws
two lines of wake behind it
on the bay like a delta
with a melted base. Sandy
billows, or so they look,
of feathery ripe heads of grass,
an acid-yellow kind of
goldenrod glowing or glowering
in shade. Rocks with rags
of shadow, washed dust clouts
that will never bleach.
It is not like this at all.
The rapid running of the
lapping water a hollow knock
of someone shipping oars:
it's eleven years since
Frank sat at this desk and
saw and heard it all
the incessant water the
immutable crickets only
not the same: new needles
on the spruce, new seaweed
on the low-tide rocks
other grass and other water
even the great gold lichen
on a granite boulder
even the boulder quite
literally is not the same

II

A day subtle and suppressed
in mounds of juniper enfolding
scratchy pockets of shadow
while bigness—rocks, trees, a stump—
stand shadowless in an overcast
of ripe grass. There is nothing
but shade, like the boggy depths
of a stand of spruce, its resonance
just the thin scream
of mosquitoes ascending.
Boats are light lumps on the bay
stretching past erased islands
to ocean and the terrible tumble
and London ("rain persisting")
and Paris ("changing to rain").
Delicate day, setting the bright
of a young spruce against the cold
of an old one hung with unripe cones
each exuding at its tip
gum, pungent, clear as a tear,
a day tarnished and fractured
as the quartz in the rocks
of a dulled and distant point,
a day like a gull passing
with a slow flapping of wings
in a kind of lope, without
breeze enough to shake loose
the last of the fireweed flowers,
a faintly clammy day, like wet silk
stained by one dead branch
the harsh russet of dried blood.

Empathy and New Year

*A notion like that of empathy inspires great distrust in us, because it
connotes a further dose of irrationalism and mysticism.*

Lévi-Strauss

I

Whitman took the cars
all the way from Camden
and when he got here
or rather there, said,
"Quit quoting," and took the next
back, through the Jersey meadows
which were that then. But
what if it is all, "Maya,
illusion?" I
doubt it, though. Men are not
so inventive. Or
few are. Not knowing
a name for something proves nothing. Right
now it isn't raining, snowing, sleeting, slushing,
yet it is
doing something. As a matter of fact
it is raining snow. Snow
from cold clouds
that melts as it strikes.
To look out a window is to sense
wet feet. Now to infuse
the garage with a subjective state
and can't make it seem to
even if it is a little like
What the Dentist Saw
a dark gullet with gleams and red.
"You come to me at midnight"
and say, "I can smell that after-
Christmas letdown coming like a hound."
And clarify, "I can smell it
just like a hound does."
So it came. It's a shame
expectations are
so often to be counted on.

New Year is nearly here
and who, knowing himself, would
endanger his desires
resolving them
in a formula? After a while
even a wish flashing by
as a thought provokes a
knock on wood so often
a little dish-like place
worn in this desk just holds
a lucky stone inherited
from an unlucky man. Nineteen-sixty-
eight: what a lovely name
to give a year. Even better
than the dogs': Wert
(". . . bird thou never . . .")
and Woofy. Personally
I am going to call
the New Year, Mutt.
Flattering it
will get you nowhere.

II

Awake at four and heard
a snowplow not rumble—
a huge beast
at its chow and wondered
is it 1968 or 1969?
for a bit. 1968 had
such a familiar sound.
Got coffee and started
reading Darwin: so modest,
so innocent, so pleased at
the surprise that *he*
should grow up to be *him*. How
grand to begin a new
year with a new writer
you really love. A snow
shovel scrapes: it's
twelve hours later
and the sun that came

so late is almost gone:
a few pink minutes and
yet the days get
longer. Coming from the
movies last night snow
had fallen in almost
still air and lay
on all, so all twigs
were emboldened to
make big disclosures.
It felt warm, warm
that is for cold
the way it does
when snow falls without
wind. "A snow picture," you
said, under the clung-to
elms, "worth painting." I
said, "The weather operator
said, 'Turning tomorrow
to bitter cold.'" "Then
the wind will veer round
to the north and blow
all of it down." Maybe I
thought it will get cold
some other way. You
as usual were right.
It did and has. Night
and snow and the threads of life
for once seen as they are,
in ropes like roots.

An East Window on Elizabeth Street

for Bob Dash

Among the silvery, the dulled sparkling mica lights of tar roofs
lie rhizomes of wet under an iris
from a bargain nursery sky: a feeble blue with skim milk blotched
on the falls. Junky buildings, aligned by a child
("That's very good, dear") are dental:
carious, and the color of weak gums ("Rinse and spit"
and blood-stained sputum and big gritty bits
are swirled away). Across an interstice
trundle and trot trucks, cabs, cars,
station-bound fat dressy women
("I never thought I'd make it")
all foundation garments and pinched toes. I don't know how
it can look so miraculous and alive
an organic skin for the stacked cubes of air
people need, things forcing up through the thick unwilling air
obstinate and mindless as the glorious swamp flower
skunk cabbage and the tight uncurling punchboard slips
of fern fronds. Toned, like patched, wash-faded rags.
Noble and geometric, like Laurana's project for a square.
Mutable, delicate, expendable, ugly, mysterious
(seven stories of just bathroom windows)
packed: a man asleep, a woman slicing garlic thinly into oil
(what a stink, what a wonderful smell)
burgeoning with stacks, pipes, ventilators, tensile antennae—
that bristling gray bit is a part of a bridge,
that mesh hangar on a roof is to play games under.
But why should a metal ladder climb, straight
and sky-aspiring, five rungs above a stairway hood
up into nothing? Out there
a bird is building a nest out of torn-up letters
and the red cellophane off cigarette and gum packs.
The furthest-off people are tiny as fine seed
but not at all bug-like. A pinprick of blue
plainly is a child running.

A Gray Thought

In the sky a gray thought
ponders on three kinds of green:
Brassy tarnished leaves of lilacs
holding on half-heartedly and long
after most turned and fell to make
a scatter rug, warmly, brightly brown.
Odd, that the tattered heart-shapes
on a Persian shrub should stay
as long as the northern needles
of the larch. Near, behind the lilac,
on a trunk, pale Paris green, green
as moonlight, growing on another time scale
a slowness becoming vast as though
all the universe were an atom
of a filterable virus in a head
that turns an eye to smile
or frown or stare into other
eyes: and not of gods, but creatures
whose size begins beyond the sense of size:
lichens, softly colored, hard in durance,
a permanence like rock on a transient tree.
And another green, a dark thick green
to face the winter, laid in layers on
the spruce and balsam or in foxtail
bursts on pine in springy shapes
that weave and pierce
the leafless and unpatterned woods.

To Frank O'Hara

for Don Allen

And now the splendor of your work is here
so complete, even
"a note on the type"
yes, total, even the colophon

and now people you never met will meet
and talk about your work.
So witty, so sad,
so you: even your lines have

a broken nose. And in the crash
of certain chewed-up words
I see you again dive
into breakers! How you scared

us, no, dazzled us swimming
in an electric storm
which is what you were
more lives than a cat

dancing, you had a feline
grace, poised on the balls
of your feet ready
to dive and

all of it, your poems,
compressed into twenty years.
How you charmed, fumed,
blew smoke from your nostrils

like a race horse that
just won the race
steaming, eager to run
only you used words.

Stay up all night? Who wants to sleep?
It is not your voice I hear
it is your words I see
foam flecks and city girders

as once from a crosstown bus
I saw you waiting a cab in light rain
(drizzle) as once you
gave me a driving lesson and the radio

played *The Merry Widow.* It broke us up.
As once under the pie plate tree
(Paulonia)
it broke you up to read Sophie Tucker

—with the *Times* in a hammock—
had a gold tea service. "It's way out
on the nut," she said, "for service,
but it was my dream."

Shimmer

The pear tree that last year
was heavy-laden this year
bears little fruit. Was
it that wet spring we had?
All the pear tree leaves
go shimmer, all at once. The
August sun blasts down
into the coolness from the
ocean. *The New York Times*
is on strike. My daily
fare! I'll starve! Not
quite. On my sill, balls
of twine wrapped up in
cellophane glitter. The
brown, the white and one
I think you'd call écru.
The sunlight falls partly
in a cup: it has a blue
transfer of two boys, a
dog and a duck and says,
"Come Away Pompey." I
like that cup, half
full of sunlight. Today
you could take up the
tattered shadows off
the grass. Roll them
and stow them. And collect
the shimmerings in a
cup, like the coffee
here at my right hand.

October

Books litter the bed,
leaves the lawn. It
lightly rains. Fall has
come: unpatterned, in
the shedding leaves.

The maples ripen. Apples
come home crisp in bags.
This pear tastes good.
It rains lightly on the
random leaf patterns.

The nimbus is spread
above our island. Rain
lightly patters on un-
shed leaves. The books
of fall litter the bed.

The Bluet

And is it stamina
that unseasonably freaks
forth a bluet, a
Quaker lady, by
the lake? So small,
a drop of sky that
splashed and held,
four-petaled, creamy
in its throat. The woods
around were brown,
the air crisp as a
Carr's table water
biscuit and smelt of
cider. There were frost
apples on the trees in
the field below the house.
The pond was still, then
broke into a ripple.
The hills, the leaves that
have not yet fallen
are deep and oriental
rug colors. Brown leaves
in the woods set off
gray trunks of trees.
But that bluet was
the focus of it all: last
spring, next spring, what
does it matter? Unexpected
as a tear when someone
reads a poem you wrote
for him: "It's this line
here." That bluet breaks
me up, tiny spring flower
late, late in dour October.

Hymn to Life

The wind rests its cheek upon the ground and feels the cool damp
And lifts its head with twigs and small dead blades of grass
Pressed into it as you might at the beach rise up and brush away
The sand. The day is cool and says, "I'm just staying overnight."
The world is filled with music, and in between the music, silence
And varying the silence all sorts of sounds, natural and man-made:
There goes a plane, some cars, geese that honk and, not here, but
Not so far away, a scream so rending that to hear it is to be
Never again the same. "Why, this is hell." Out of the death breeding
Soil, here, rise emblems of innocence, snowdrops that struggle
Easily into life and hang their white enamel heads toward the dirt
And in the yellow grass are small wild crocuses from hills goats
Have cropped to barrenness. The corms come by mail, are planted,
Then do their thing: to live! To live! So natural and so hard
Hard as it seems it must be for green spears to pierce the all-but-
Frozen mold and insist that they too, like mouse-eared chickweed,
Will live. The spears lengthen, the bud appears and spreads, its
Seed capsule fattens and falls, the green turns yellowish and withers
Stretched upon the ground. In Washington, magnolias were in bud.
In Charlottesville early bulbs were up, brightening the muck. Tomorrow
Will begin another spring. No one gets many, one at a time, like a long-
Awaited letter that one day comes. But it may not say what you hoped
Or distraction robs it of what it once would have meant. Spring comes
And the winter weather, here, may hold. It is arbitrary, like the plan
Of Washington, D.C. avenues and circles in asphalt web and no
One gets younger: which is not, for the young, true, discovering new
Freedoms at twenty, a relief not to be a teen-ager anymore. One of us
Had piles, another water on the knee, a third a hernia—a strangulated
Hernia is one of life's less pleasant bits of news—and only
One, at twenty, moved easily through all the galleries to pill
Free sleep. Oh, it's not all that bad. The sun shines on my hand
And the myriad lines that crisscross tell the story of nearly fifty
Years. Sorry, it's too long to relate. Once, when I was young, I
Awoke at first light and sitting in a rocking chair watched the sun
Come up beyond the houses across the street. Another time I stood
At the cables of a liner and watched the wake turning and
Turning upon itself. Another time I woke up and in a bottle
On a chest of drawers the thoughtful doctor had left my tonsils. I
Didn't keep them. The turning of the globe is not so real to us
As the seasons turning and the days that rise out of early gray

—The world is all cut-outs then—and slip or step steadily down
The slopes of our lives where the emotions and needs sprout. "I
Need you," tree, that dominates this yard, thick-waisted, tall
And crook-branched. Its bark scales off like that which we forget:
Pain, an introduction at a party, what precisely happened umpteen
Years or days or hours ago. And that same blue jay returns, or perhaps
It is another. All jays are one to me. But not the sun which seems at
Each rising new, as though in the night it enacted death and rebirth,
As flowers seem to. The roses this June will be different roses
Even though you cut an armful and come in saying, "Here are the roses,"
As though the same blooms had come back, white freaked with red
And heavily scented. Or a cut branch of pear blooms before its time,
"Forced." Time brings us into bloom and we wait, busy, but wait   ⌐
For the unforced flow of words and intercourse and sleep and dreams
In which the past seems to portend a future which is just more
Daily life. The cat has a ripped ear. He fights, he fights all   ⌐
The tom cats all the time. There are blood gouts on a velvet seat.
Easily sponged off: but these red drops on a book of Stifter's, will
I remember and say at some future time, "Oh, yes, that was the day
Hodge had a torn ear and bled on the card table?" Poor
Hodge, battered like an old car. Silence flows into my mind. It
Is spring. It is also still really winter. Not a day when you say,
"What a beautiful spring day." A day like twilight or evening when
You think, "I meant to watch the sun set." And then comes on
To rain. "You've got to take," says the man at the store, "the rough
With the smooth." A window to the south is rough with rain-drops
That, caught in the screen, spell out untranslatable glyphs. A story
Not told: so much not understood, a sight, an insight, and you pass on,
Another day for each day is subjective and there is a totality of days ⟍
As there are as many to live it. The day lives us and in exchange   ⟩
We it: after snowball time, a month, March, of fits and starts, winds, ⟋
Rain, spring hints and wintry arrears. The weather pays its check,
Like quarreling in a D.C. hotel, "I won't quarrel about it, but I made
No local calls." Strange city, broad and desolating, monuments
Rearing up and offices like monuments and crowds lined up to see
The White House inside. "We went to see the White House. It was lovely."
Not so strange though as the cemetery with guttering flame and
Admirals and generals with bigger gravestones than the lesser fry
Below Lee's house, false marble pillars and inside all so
Everyday, in every room a shawl tossed untidily upon a chair or bed
Created no illusion of lived-in-ness. But the periwinkles do, in beds
That flatten and are starred blue-violet, a retiring flower loved,
It would seem, of the dead, so often found where they congregate. A

Quote from Aeschylus: I forget. All, all is forgotten gradually and
One wonders if these ideas that seem handed down are truly what they were?
An idea may mutate like a plant, and what was once held basic truth
Become an idle thought, like, "Shall we plant some periwinkles there
By that bush? They're so to be depended on." The wind shakes the screen
And all the raindrops on it streak and run in stems. It's colder.
The crocuses close up. The snowdrops are brushed with mud. The sky
Colors itself rosily behind gray-black and the rain falls through
The basketball hoop on a garage, streaking its backboard with further
Trails of rust, a lovely color to set with periwinkle violet-blue.
And the trees shiver and shudder in the light rain blasts from off
The ocean. The street, wet, reflects the breakup of the clouds
On its face, driving over sky with a hissing sound. The car
Slides slightly and in the west appear streaks of different green:
A lid lifted briefly on the spring. Then the moon burns through
Racing clouds, its aureole that of rings of oil on water in a harbor
Bubbling up from an exhaust. Clear the sky, beside a rim of moon
Three stars and only three and one planet. So under lilacs unleaved
Lie a clump of snowdrops and one purple crocus. Purple, a polka-dotted
Color little girls are fond of: "See my new dress!" and she twirls
On one foot. Then, crossed, bursts into tears. Smiles and rain, like
These passing days in which buds swell, unseen as yet, waiting
For the elms to color their furtheroutmost twigs, only the willow
Gleams yellow. Life is hard. Some are strong, some weak, most
Untested. These useless truths blow about the yard the day after
Rain the soft sunlight making softer shadows on the faded lawn.
The world looks so old in the spring, laid out under the sky. One
Gull coasts by, unexpected as a kiss on the nape of the neck. These
Days need birds and so they come, a flock of ducks, and a bunch of
Small fluffy unnamed balls that hide in hedges and make a racket.
"The gift of life," as though, existing in expectancy and then
Someone came up and said, "Here," or, "Happy Birthday." It is more
Mysterious than that, pierced by blue or running in the rain
Or simply lying down to read. Writing a postponed letter which may
Bring no pleasure: arduous truths to tell. And if you thought March was bad
Consider April, early April, wet snow falling into blue squills
That underneath a beech make an illusory lake, a haze of blue
With depth to it. That is like pain, ordinary household pain,
Like piles, or bumping against a hernia. All the signs are set for A-OK.
A day to visit the National Gallery—Velásquez, Degas—but, and
What a but, with water on the knee "You'll need a wheelchair, Mummy."
Coasting among the masterpieces, of what use are they? *Angel with a
Hurdy-Gurdy* or this young man in dun clothes who holds his hat so that

The red lining shows and glows. And in the sitting room people sit
And rest their feet and talk of where they've been, motels and Monticello,
Dinner in the Fiji Room. Someone forgets a camera. Each day forgetting:
What is there so striking to remember? The rain stops. April shines
A little, stormily, the ocean off there makes its freight-car noise
Or rattles with catarrh and asks to have its nose wiped. Gray descends.
An illuminous penetration of unbright light that seeps and coats
The ragged lawn and spells out bare spots and winter fallen branches.
Yardwork. And now the yardwork is over (it is never over), today's
Stint anyway. Odd jobs, that stretch ahead, wide and mindless as
Pennsylvania Avenue or the bridge to Arlington, crossed and recrossed
And there the Lincoln Memorial crumbles. It looks so solid: it won't
Last. The impermanence of permanence, is that all there is? To look
And see the plane tree, its crooked branches brush the ground, rear
In its age, older than any of us, destined, if all goes well with it,
To outlast us all. Does one then resent the plane tree, host
To cardinals? I hear them call. Plaintively, in the mating season.
Why should a white city dog my thoughts? Vast, arid, a home to many,
So strange in its unamiability. Stony city laid out on an heroic plan,
Why are you there? Various answers present themselves, likely
As squills. It doesn't really matter, for instance, to miss the spring.
For this is spring, this mud and swelling fruit-tree buds, furred
On the apple trees. And yet it still might snow: it's been known
Falling like cherry blossom petals around the Reflecting Pool, a sight
To see. And there are sights to hear, music from a phonograph, pop
Or classical, please choose one or both. It doesn't matter. What matters
Is how the light becomes entrapped in a dusty screen, masking out
The view into the depths of the garage where cars are stalled like oxen.
Day, suddenly sunny and warming up for more, I would like to stroke you
As one strokes a cat and feels the ridgy skull beneath the fur and tickles
It behind its ears. The cat twists its head and moves it toward your fingers
Like the lifting thighs of someone fucked, moving up to meet the stroke.
The sun strokes all now in this zone, reaching in through windows to jell
Glue in jars (that takes time)—may I send you a warmed bottle of Pliobond?
It is on this desk and—here's the laugh—I don't know who put it there.
"This is something he will like, or use." Meantime, those branches go
Ungathered up. I hate fussing with nature and would like the world to be
All weeds. I see it from the train, citybound, how the yuccas and chicory
Thrive. So much messing about, why not leave the world alone? Then
There would be no books, which is not to be borne. Willa Cather alone is worth
The price of admission to the horrors of civilization. Let's make a list.
The greatest paintings. Preferred orchestral conductors. Nostalgia singers.
The best, the very best, roses. After learning all their names—Rose

de Rescht, Cornelia, Pax—it is important to forget them. All these
Lists are so much dirty laundry. Sort it out fast and send to laundry
Or hurl into washing machine, add soap and let'er spin. The truth is
That all these household tasks and daily work—up the street two men
Install an air conditioner—are beautiful. Flowers and machines that people
Love: the boy who opts for trade school while white-collar kids
Call him a greaser. I wish I could take an engine apart and reassemble it.
I also wish I sincerely wanted to. I don't. "Love is everything that it's
Cracked up to be." There's a song for you. Another is in the silence
Of a windless day. Hear it? Motors, yes, and the scrabbling of the surf
But, too, the silence in which out of the muck arise violet leaves
(Leaves of violets, that is). The days slide by and we feel we must
Stamp an impression on them. It is quite other. They stamp us, both
Time and season so that looking back there are wide unpeopled avenues
Blue-gray with cars on them, parked either side, and a small bridge that
Crosses Rock Creek has four bison at its corners, out of scale
Yet so mysterious to childhood, friendly, ominous, pattable because
Of bronze. The rain comes back, this spring, like a thirsty dog
Who goes back and back to his dish. "Fill it up, please," wag wag.
Gray depression and purple shadows, the daffodils feigning sunlight
That came yesterday. One day rain, one day sun, the weather is stuck
Like a record. Through it all the forsythia begins to bloom, brown
And yellow and warm as lit gas jets, clinging like bees to
The arching canes where starlings take cover from foraging cats. Not
To know: what have these years of living and being lived taught us?
Not to quarrel? Scarcely. You want to shoot pool, I want to go home:
And just before the snap of temper one had sensed so
Strongly the pleasure of watching a game well played: the cue ball
Carom and the struck ball pocketed. Skill. And still the untutored
Rain comes down. Open the laundry door. Press your face into the
Wet April chill: a life mask. Attune yourself to what is happening
Now, the little wet things, like washing up the lunch dishes. Bubbles
Rise, rinse and it is done. Let the dishes air-dry, the way
You let your hair after a shampoo. All evaporates, water, time, the
Happy moments and—harder to believe—the unhappy. Time on a bus,
That passes, and the night with its burthen and gift of dreams. That
Other life we live and need, filled with joys and terrors, threaded
By dailiness: where the wished-for sometimes happens, or, just
Before waking tremulous hands undo buttons. Another day, the sun
Comes out from behind unbuttoned cloud underclothes—gray with use—
And bud scales litter the sidewalks. A new shop is being built,
An old one refurbished. What was a white interior will now be brown
Behind men's clothes, there are these changes in taste. Fashion

It anew. Change in everything yet none so great as the changes in
Oneself, which, short of sickness, go unobserved. Why watch
Yourself? You know you're here, and where tomorrow you probably will
Be. In the delicatessen a woman made a fumbling gesture then
Slowly folded toward the floor. "Get a doctor," someone said. "She's
Having a fit." Not knowing how to help I left, taking with me
The look of appeal in faded blue eyes. Between these sharp attacks
Of harsh reality I would like to interpose: interpose is not the
Word. One wants them not to happen, that's all, but, like slammed-
On brakes—the cab skids, you are thrown forward, ouch—they
Come. Times when religion would help: "Be merciful" "Intercede"
"That which I should have done . . ." Fear and superstition and some-
Thing more. But without the conviction of a truth, best leave
It alone. Life, it seems, explains nothing about itself. In the ⟩
Garden now daffodils stand full unfolded and to see them is enough.
They seem no more passing than when they weren't there: perhaps
The promise when first the blades pierced the wintry soil
Was better? You see, you invent choices where none exist. Perhaps
It is not a choice but a preference? No, take it all, it's free,
Help yourself. The sap rises. The trees leaf out and bloom. You
Suddenly sense: you don't know what. An exhilaration that revives
Old views and surges of energy or the pure pleasure of
Simply looking. A car goes over a rise and there are birches snow
Twisted into cabalistic shapes: The Devil's Notch; or Smuggler's
Gap. At the time you could not have imagined the time when you
Would forget the name, as apparent and there as your own. Rivers
Reflecting silver skies, how many boys have swum in you? A rope
Tied to a tree caught between my thighs and I was yanked headfirst
And fell into the muddy creek. What a long time it seemed, rising
To the surface, how lucky it didn't catch me in the groin. That
Won't happen twice, I imagine. That summer sun was the same
As this April one: is repetition boring? Or only inactivity? Quite ⟩
A few things are boring, like the broad avenues of Washington,
D.C., that seem to go from nowhere and back again. Civil servants
Wait at the crossing to cross to lunch at the Waffle House. In
This twilight Degas a woman sits and holds a fan, it's
The just rightness that counts. And how have you come to know just
Rightness when you see it and what is the deep stirring that it
Brings? Art is as mysterious as nature, as life, of which it is
A flower. Under the hedges now the weedy strips grow bright
With dandelions, just as good a flower as any other. Unfortunately,
You can't pick them: they wilt. But these burgeoning days are
Not like any others. Promise is a part of it, promise of warmth

And vegetative growth. "Wheel me out into the sun, Sonny,
These old bones that creak need it." And the gardener does not
Come back: over the winter he had a heart attack, has to take it
Easy. You see death shadowed out in another's life. The threat
Is always there, even in balmy April sunshine. So what
If it is hard to believe in? Stopping in the city while the light
Is red, to think that all who stop with you too must stop, and
Yet it is not less individual a fate for all that. "When I
was born, death kissed me. I kissed it back." Meantime, there
Is bridge, and solitaire, and phone calls and a door slams, someone
Goes out into the April sun to take a spin as far as the
Grocer's, to shop, and then come back. In the fullness of time,
Let me hand you an empty cup, coffee-stained. Or a small glass
Of spirits: "Here's your ounce of whisky for today." Next door
The boys dribble a basketball and practice shots. Two boys
Run by: high spirits. The postman comes. No mail of interest.
Another day, there is. A postcard of the Washington Monument,
A friend waving from a small window at the needle top. "Hoo
Hoo" he calls. Another day, and still the sun shines down, warming
Tulips into bloom, a redder red than blood. The dandelions
Cringe before them. In the evening there will be time enough
To drive from here to there, study the vegetable patch, admire
The rosy violets. Life in action, life in repose, life in
Contemplation, which is hard to tell from daydreaming, on a day
When the sky woolgathers clouds and sets their semblance on a
Glassy ocean. Only its edge goes lisp. On no two days the same.
Is it the ocean's mindlessness that troubles? At times it seems
Calculatedly malevolent, tearing the dunes asunder, tumbling
Summer houses into itself, a terror to see. They say there are
Those who have never felt terror. A slight creeping of the scalp,
Merely. How fine. Finer than sand, that, on a day like this,
Trickles through my fingers, ensconced in a dune cleft, sun-
Warmed and breeze-cooled. This peace is full of sounds and
Movement. A couple passes, jogging. A dog passes, barking
And running. My nose runs, a little. Just a drip. Left over
From winter. How long ago it seems! All spring and summer stretch
Ahead, a roadway lined by roses and thunder. "It will be here
Before you know it." These twigs will then have leafed and
Shower down a harvest of yellow-brown. So far away, so
Near at hand. The sand runs through my fingers. The yellow
Daffodils have white corollas (sepals?). The crocuses are gone,
I didn't see them go. They were here, now they're not. Instead
The forsythia ensnarls its flames, cool fire, pendent above the smoke

Of its brown branches. Beaches are near. It rains again: the screen
And window glass are pebbled by it. It soaks through a raincoat that
Has had its water repellency dry-cleaned out of it. Most modern
Inventions don't work so well, or not for long. A breakdown occurs,
Or something simple, like the dishwasher detergent eating off
The pattern on china, even the etched florets on wineglasses.
Strong stuff. From the train, a stand of larch is greener than
Greenest grass. A funny tree, of many moods, gold in autumn, naked
In winter: an evergreen (it looks) that isn't. What kind of a tree
Is that? I love to see it resurrect itself, the enfolded buttons
Of needles studding the branches, then opening into little bursts.
And that Washington flower, the pink magnolia tree, blooms now
In little yards, its trunk a smoky gray. And soon the hybrid azaleas,
So much too much, will follow, and the tender lilac. Persia, we
Have much to thank you for, besides the word lapis lazuli. And someone
You know well is suffering, sees it all but not the way before
Him, hating his job and not knowing what to change it for. Have
You any advice to give? Have you learned nothing in all these
Years? "Take it as it comes." Sit still and listen: each so alone.
Someone driving decides not to take that curve, to pile it up
In smithereens, the anxious and unsatisfying years: goodbye, life.
Others keep on living so as not to wound their friends: the suicide
Fantasy, to awaken rested and fresh, to plunge into a deep and
Dreamless sleep, to be mindless and at one with all that grows,
Dies and revives each April, here, crying, "Stir your stumps!"
In the mental hospital a patient is ready to be discharged. "I'm
So glad to be going home!" Where the same old problems wait;
Still, to feel more equal to them, that's something. "Time heals
All wounds": now what's that supposed to mean? Wounds can
Kill, like that horse-chestnut tree with the rotting place will surely
Die unless the tree doctor comes. Cut out the rot, fill with tree
Cement, score and leave to heal. The rain comes down in buckets:
I've never seen that, though you often speak of it. The rain
Comes down and brings depression, too much and too often. And there
Is the fog off the cold Atlantic. No one is at his best with
A sinus headache. It will pass. Stopped passages unblock: why
Let the lovely spring, its muck and scarlet emperors, get you
Down. Unhibernate. Let the rain soak your hair, run down your
Face, hang in drops from facial protuberances. Face into
It, then towel dry. Then another day brings back the sun and
Violets in the grass. The pear tree thickens all its boughs and
Twigs into silver-white, a dimmed brilliance, and already at
Its base a circle of petals on the unmowed grass. Far away

In Washington, at the Reflecting Pool, the Japanese cherries
Bust out into their dog mouth pink. Visitors gasp. The sun
Drips, coats and smears, all that spring yellow under unending
Blue. Only the oaks hold back their leaf buds, reticent.
Reticence is not a bad quality, though it may lead to misunderstandings.
I misunderstood silence for disapproval, see now it was
Sympathy. Thank you, May, for these warm stirrings. Life
Goes on, it seems, though in all sorts of places—nursing
Homes—it is drawing to a close. Abstractions and generalities:
Grass and blue depths into which the evening star seems set.
As windows are set in walls in whited Washington. City, begone
From my thoughts: childhood was not all that gay. Nor all that gray,
For the matter of that. May leans in my window, offering hornets.
To them too I give leave to go about their business, which is not
Nesting in my books. The fresh-mown lawn is a rug underneath
Which is swept the dirt, the living dirt out of which our nurture
Comes, to which we go, not knowing if we hasten or we tarry. May
Opens wide her bluest eyes and speaks in bird tongues and a
Chain saw. The blighted elms come down. Already maple saplings,
Where elms once grew and whelmed, count as young trees. In
A dishpan the soap powder dissolves under a turned-on faucet and
Makes foam, like the waves that crash ashore at the foot
Of the street. A restless surface. Chewing, and spitting sand and
Small white pebbles, clam shells with a sheen or chalky white.
A horseshoe crab: primeval. And all this without thought, this
Churning energy. Energy! The sun sucks up the dew; the day is
Clear; a bird shits on my window ledge. Rain will wash it off
Or a storm will chip it loose. Life, I do not understand.
Days tick by, each so unique, each so alike: what is that chatter
In the grass? May is not a flowering month so much as shades
Of green, yellow-green, blue-green, or emerald or dusted like
The lilac leaves. The lilac trusses stand in bud. A cardinal
Passes like a flying tulip, alights and nails the green day
Down. One flame in a fire of sea-soaked, copper-fed wood:
A red that leaps from green and holds it there. Reluctantly
The plane tree, always late, as though from age, opens up and
Hangs its seed balls out. The apples flower. The pear is past.
Winter is suddenly so far away, behind, ahead. From the train
A stand of coarse grass in fuzzy flower. Is it for miracles
We live? I love it when the morning sun lights up my room
Like a yellow jelly bean, an inner glow. May mutters, "Why
ask questions?" or, "What are the questions you wish to ask?"

June 30, 1974

for Jane and Joe Hazan

Let me tell you
that this weekend Sunday
morning in the country
fills my soul
with tranquil joy:
the dunes beyond
the pond beyond
the humps of bayberry—
my favorite
shrub (today,
at least)—are
silent as a mountain
range: such a
subtle profile
against a sky that
goes from dawn
to blue. The roses
stir, the grapevine
at one end of the deck
shakes and turns
its youngest leaves
so they show pale
and flower-like.
A redwing blackbird
pecks at the grass;
another perches on a bush.
Another way, a millionaire's
white château turns
its flank to catch
the risen sun. No
other houses, except
this charming one,
alive with paintings,
plants and quiet.
I haven't said
a word. I like
to be alone
with friends. To get up

to this morning view
and eat poached eggs
and extra toast with
Tiptree Gooseberry Preserve
(green)—and coffee,
milk, no sugar. Jane
said she heard
the freeze-dried kind
is healthier when
we went shopping
yesterday and she
and John bought
crude blue Persian plates.
How can coffee be
healthful? I mused
as sunny wind
streamed in the car
window driving home.
Home! How lucky to
have one, how arduous
to make this scene
of beauty for
your family and
friends. Friends!
How we must have
sounded, gossiping at
the dinner table
last night. Why, *that*
dinner table is
this breakfast table:
"The boy in trousers
is not the same boy
in no trousers," who
said? Discontinuity
in all we see and are:
the same, yet change,
change, change. "Inez,
it's good to see you."
Here comes the cat, sedate,
that killed and brought
a goldfinch yesterday.
I'd like to go out
for a swim but

it's a little cool
for that. Enough to
sit here drinking coffee,
writing, watching the clear
day ripen (such
a rainy June we had)
while Jane and Joe
sleep in their room
and John in his. I
think I'll make more toast.

Korean Mums

beside me in this garden
are huge and daisy-like
(why not? are not
oxeye daisies a chrysanthemum?),
shrubby and thick-stalked,
the leaves pointing up
the stems from which
the flowers burst in
sunbursts. I love
this garden in all its moods,
even under its winter coat
of salt hay, or now,
in October, more than
half gone over: here
a rose, there a clump
of aconite. This morning
one of the dogs killed
a barn owl. Bob saw
it happen, tried to
intervene. The airedale
snapped its neck and left
it lying. Now the bird
lies buried by an apple
tree. Last evening
from the table we saw
the owl, huge in the dusk,
circling the field
on owl-silent wings.
The first one ever seen
here: now it's gone,
a dream you just remember.

The dogs are barking. In
the studio music plays
and Bob and Darragh paint.
I sit scribbling in a little
notebook at a garden table,
too hot in a heavy shirt
in the mid-October sun
into which the Korean mums

all face. There is a
dull book with me,
an apple core, cigarettes,
an ashtray. Behind me
the rue I gave Bob
flourishes. Light on leaves,
so much to see, and
all I really see is that
owl, its bulk troubling
the twilight. I'll
soon forget it: what
is there I have not forgot?
Or one day will forget:
this garden, the breeze
in stillness, even
the words, Korean mums.

Wystan Auden

I went to his fortieth birthday
party: was it really twenty-seven
years ago? I don't remember what
street he was living on, but he
was adapting *The Duchess of Malfi*:
Canada Lee appeared in white face:
it was that long ago. It was in
that apartment I just missed
meeting Brecht and T.S. Eliot.

I remember Chester so often saying,
"Oh *Wystan*!" while Wystan looked
pleased at having stirred him up.

On Ischia he claimed to take
St. Restituta seriously, and
sat at Maria's café in the cobbled
square saying, "Poets should
dress like businessmen," while
he wore an incredible peach-
colored nylon shirt. And on
Fire Island his telling someone,
"You must write each book as
though it were your last." And
when he learned that in Florence
I and my friend Bill Aalto had
fished his drafts of poems
out of the wastepaper basket,
he took to burning them, saying,
"I feel like an ambassador burning
secret papers." When he got off
the liner at Naples, in black and
a homburg, he said, "I've just
read *all* of Doughty's *The Dawn
in Britain*." And earlier, right
after the war, "My dear, I'm the
first major poet to have flown
the Atlantic." He was very kind.
Once, when I had an operation
in Rome, he wrote me quite a large

check: I forget for how much.
When I sent it back and asked
for (for a more favorable ex-
change on the black market)
cash, he sent it, along with
a cross note saying he was
a busy man. Once when a group
of us made an excursion from
Ischia—Capri, Sorrento, Positano,
Amalfi, Pompeii—he suddenly
said at cocktails on a pensione
terrace: "More of this sitting
around like beasts!" He was
industrious, writing away in
a smoky room—fug—in a
ledger or on loose sheets
poems, some of which I typed
for him (they're in *Nones*).

I don't have to burn his
letters as he asked his
friends to do: they were lost
a long time ago. So much
to remember, so little to
say: that he liked martinis
and was greedy about the wine?
I always thought he would live
to a great age. He did not.
Wystan, kind man, great poet,
goodbye.

Dining Out with Doug and Frank

for Frank Polach

Not quite yet. First,
around the corner for a visit
to the Bella Landauer Collection
of printed ephemera:
luscious lithos and why did
Fairy Soap vanish and
Crouch and Fitzgerald survive?
Fairy Soap was once a
household word! I've been living
at Broadway and West 74th
for a week and still haven't
ventured on a stroll in
Central Park, two bizarre blocks
away. (Bizarre is for the ex-
town houses, mixing Byzantine
with Gothic and Queen Anne.)
My abstention from the park
is for Billy Nichols who went
bird-watching there and, for
his binoculars, got his
head beat in. Streaming blood,
he made it to an avenue
where no cab would pick him up
until one did and at
Roosevelt Hospital he waited
several hours before any
doctor took him in hand. A
year later he was dead. But
I'll make the park: I carry
more cash than I should and
walk the street at night
without feeling scared unless
someone scary passes.

II

Now it's tomorrow,
as usual. Turned out that
Doug (Douglas Crase, the poet)
had to work (he makes his bread
writing speeches): thirty pages
explaining why Eastman Kodak's
semi-slump (?) is just what
the stockholders ordered. He
looked glum, and declined
a drink. By the by did you know
that John Ashbery's grandfather
was offered an investment-in
when George Eastman founded his
great corporation? He turned it
down. Eastman Kodak will survive.
"Yes" and where would our
John be now? I can't imagine him
any different than he is,
a problem which does not arise,
so I went with Frank (the poet,
he makes his dough as a librarian,
botanical librarian at Rutgers
and as a worker he's a beaver:
up at 5:30, home after 7, but
over striped bass he said he
had begun to see the unwisdom
of his ways and next week will
revert to the seven-hour day
for which he's paid. Good. Time
and energy to write. Poetry
takes it out of you, or you
have to have a surge to bring
to it. Words. So useful and
pleasant) to dine at McFeely's
at West 23rd and Eleventh Avenue
by the West River, which is
the right name for the Hudson
when it bifurcates from
the East River to create
Manhattan "an isle of joy."
Take my word for it, don't

(shall I tell you about my
friend who effectively threw
himself under a train in
the Times Square station?
No. Too tender to touch. In
fact, at the moment I've blocked
out his name. No I haven't:
Peter Kemeny, gifted and tormented
fat man) listen to anyone
else.

III

Oh. At the Battery all
that water becomes the
North River, which seems
to me to make no sense
at all. I always thought
Castle Garden faced Calais.

IV

Peconic Bay scallops, the
tiny, the real ones and cooked
in butter, not breaded and
plunged in deep grease. The food
is good and reasonable (for these
days) but the point is McFeely's
itself—the owner's name or
was it always called that? It's
the bar of the old Terminal Hotel
and someone (McFeely?) has had
the wit to restore it to what
it was: all was there, under
layers of paint and abuse, neglect.
You, perhaps, could put a date
on it: I'll vote for 1881
or the 70's. The ceiling is
florid glass, like the cabbage-rose
runners in the grand hotels
at Saratoga: when were they built?

The bar is thick and long and
sinuous, virile. Mirrors: are
the decorations on them cut
or etched? I do remember that
above the men's room door the
word Toilet is etched
on a transom. Beautiful lettering,
but nothing to what lurks
within: the three most
splendid urinals I've ever
seen. Like Roman steles. I
don't know what I was going
to say. Yes. Does the Terminal Hotel
itself still function? (Did you
know that "they" sold all the
old mirror glass out of Gage
and Tollner's? Donald Droll has
a fit every time he eats there.)
"Terminal," I surmise, because
the hotel faced the terminal
of the 23rd Street ferry, a
perfect sunset sail to Hoboken
and the yummies of the Clam
Broth House, which, thank God,
still survives. Not many do:
Gage and Tollner's, the Clam Broth House,
McSorley's and now McFeely's. Was
that the most beautiful of the
ferry houses or am I thinking
of Christopher Street? And there
was another uptown that crossed
to Jersey and back but docking
further downtown: it sailed
on two diagonals. And wasn't
there one at 42nd? It couldn't
matter less, they're gone, all
gone and we are left with just
the Staten Island ferry, all
right in its way but how often
do you want to pass Miss Liberty
and see that awesome spiky postcard
view? The river ferryboats were
squat and low like tugs, old

and wooden and handsome, you
were *in* the water, *in* the shipping:
Millay wrote a poem about
it all. I cannot accept their
death, or any other death. Bill
Aalto, my first lover (five tumultuous
years found Bill chasing me around
the kitchen table—in Wystan Auden's
house in Forio d'Ischia—with
a carving knife. He was serious
and so was I and so I wouldn't go
when he wanted to see me when
he was dying of leukemia. Am I
sorry? Not really. The fear had
gone too deep. The last time I
saw him was in the City Center lobby
and he was jolly—if he just
stared at you and the tears began
it was time to cut and run—
and the cancer had made him lose
a lot of weight and he looked
young and handsome as the night
we picked each other up
in Pop Tunick's long-gone gay bar.
Bill never let me forget that
on the jukebox I kept playing
Lena Horne's "Mad about the Boy."
Why the nagging teasing? It's
a great performance but he
thought it was East Fifties queen
taste. Funny—or, funnily enough—
in dreams, and I dream about him
a lot, he's always the nice guy
I first knew and loved, not
the figure of terror he became.
Oh well. Bill had his hour: he
was a hero, a major in the
Abraham Lincoln Brigade. A dark
Finn who looked not unlike
a butch version of Valentino.
Watch out for Finns. They're
murder when they drink) used
to ride the ferries all the

time, doing the bars along
the waterfront: did you know
Hoboken has—or had—
more bars (Death.
At least twice when
someone I knew and hated
died I felt the joy of vengeance:
I mean I smiled and laughed out
loud: a hateful feeling.
It passes) to the square inch
than any other city? "Trivia,
Goddess . . ." Through dinner
I wanted to talk more than we
did about Frank's poems. All it
came down to was "experiment
more," "try collages," and "write
some skinny poems" but I like
where he's heading now and
Creative Writing has never
been my trip although I understand
the fun of teaching someone
/ something fun to do although most people
⟨ simply have not got the gift
\ and where's the point? What
puzzles me is what my friends
find to say. Oh, forget it. Reading,
writing, knowing other poets
will do it, if there is
anything doing. The reams
of shit I've read. It would
have been so nice after dinner
to take a ferry boat with Frank
across the Hudson (or West River,
if you prefer). To be on
the water in the dark and
the wonder of electricity—
the real beauty of Manhattan.
Oh well. When they tore down
the Singer Building,
and when I saw the Bogardus Building
rusty and coming unstitched in
a battlefield of rubble I deliberately
/ withdrew my emotional investments

in loving old New York. Except
you can't. I really like
dining out and last night was
especially fine. A full moon
when we parted hung over
Frank and me. Why is this poem
so long? And full of death?
Frank and Doug are young and
beautiful and have nothing
to do with that. Why is this poem
so long? "Enough is as good
as a feast" and I'm a Herrick fan.
I'd like to take that plunge
into Central Park, only I'm
waiting for Darragh Park to phone.
Oh. Doug and Frank. One is light,
the other dark.
Doug is the tall one.

The Payne Whitney Poems

TRIP

Wigging in, wigging out:
when I stop to think
the wires in my head
cross: kaboom. How
many trips
by ambulance (five,
count them five),
claustrated, pill addiction,
in and out of mental
hospitals,
the suicidalness (once
I almost made it)
but—I go on?
Tell you all of it?
I can't. When I think
of that, that at
only fifty-one I,
Jim the Jerk, am
still alive and breathing
deeply, that I think
is a miracle.

WE WALK

in the garden. Sun
on the river
flashing past. I
dig ivy leaves.
We walk in a
maze. Sun, shine
on. Now it is
one hour later.
Out the window no
sun. Cloud
turbulence and
the wind whistles.
Curious.

ARCHES

of buildings, this building,
frame a stream of windows
framed in white brick. This
building is fireproof; or else
it isn't: the furnishings first
to go: no, the patients. Patients
on Sundays walk in a small garden.
Today some go out on a group
pass. To stroll the streets and shop.
So what else is new? The sky
slowly/swiftly went blue to gray.
A gray in which some smoke stands.

LINEN

Is this the moment?
No, not yet.
When is the
moment?
Perhaps there is
none.
Need I persist?

This morning I
changed bedding.
At lunch I watched
someone shake out
the tablecloth, fold
and stow it in a side-
board. Then, the
cigarette moment.
Now, this moment
flows out of me
down the pen and
writes.

I'm glad I have
fresh linen.

HEATHER AND CALENDULAS

A violet hush: and sunbursts.
An aluminum measure
full of water. Scentlessness.
"Go to church next week?"
Fortuitous as nuts too
salty. Accordion pleats.
The phone bill is buff.
Three postcards of three
paintings. A good review.
Pale green walls and
a white ceiling. Lamps
lit in daylight. Ice.
The temperature 16. In
February. "Laugh and
the world laughs with you."
Die, and you die alone.

BACK

from the Frick. The weather
cruel as Henry Clay himself.
Who put that collection together?
Duveen? I forget. It was nice
to see the masterpieces again,
covered with the strikers' blood.
What's with art anyway, that
we give it such precedence?
I love the paintings, that's for sure.
What I really loved today
was New York, its streets and
men selling flowers and hot dogs,
mysterious town houses,
the gritty wind. I used to live
around here but it's changed some.
Why? That was only thirty years ago.

BLIZZARD

Tearing and tearing
ripped-up bits of paper,
no, it's not paper
it's snow. Blown side-
ways in the wind,
coming in my window
wetting stacked books.
"Mr Park called. He
can't come visiting
today." Of course not,
in this driving icy
weather. How I wish
I were out in it! A
figure like an ex-
clamation point seen
through driving snow.

FEBRUARY 13, 1975

Tomorrow is St Valentine's:
tomorrow I'll think about
that. Always nervous, even
after a good sleep I'd like
to climb back into. The sun
shines on yesterday's new-
fallen snow and yesteereven
it turned the world to pink
and rose and steel-blue
buildings. Helene is restless:
leaving soon. And what then
will I do with myself? Some-
one is watching morning
TV. I'm not reduced to that
yet. I wish one could press
snowflakes in a book like flowers.

SLEEP

The friends who come to see you
and the friends who don't.
The weather in the window.
A pierced ear.
The mounting tension and the spasm.
A paper-lace doily on a small plate.
Tangerines.
A day in February: heart-
shaped cookies on St Valentine's.
Like Christopher, a discarded saint.
A tough woman with black hair.
"I got to set my wig straight."
A gold and silver day begins to wane.
A crescent moon.
Ice on the window.
Give my love to, oh, anybody.

PASTIME

I pick up a loaded pen and twiddle it.
After the blizzard
cold days of shrinking snow.
At visiting hour the cars
below my window form up
in a traffic jam. A fast-
moving man is in charge,
herding the big machines
like cattle. Weirdly, it all
keeps moving somehow. I read
a dumb detective story. I
clip my nails: hard
as iron or glass. The clippers
keep sliding off them. Today
I'm shaky. A shave, a bath.
Chat. The morning paper.
Sitting. Staring. Thinking blankly.
TV. A desert kind of life.

WHAT

What's in those pills?
After lunch and I can
hardly keep my eyes
open. Oh, for someone
to
talk small talk with.
Even a dog would do.

Why are they hammering
iron outside? And what
is that generator whose
fierce hum comes in
the window? What is a
poem, anyway.

The daffodils, the heather
and the freesias all
speak to me, I speak
back, like St Francis
and the wolf of Gubbio.

The Snowdrop

The sheath pierces the turf
and the flower unfurls: drooping,
pendent, white, three-petaled,
the corolla with a frill
of green: the virgin of the spring!
In earliest spring! (Reginald
Farrer hated snowdrops: in his
Yorkshire rock garden the rain
beat them down into the mud
and they got all dirty. Why not
pick a few, wash them off and
make a nosegay in a wineglass,
Reginald?) And when the flower
fades and dies, the stem
measures its length along the sod,
the seed pod swelling like
a pale green testicle.

En Route to Southampton

In a corner of a parlor-car
window, a thin crescent is
the moon. Below,
the sky on the horizon
is oily bilge.
The leafless trees go by,
the ugly houses,
the parlor car
is much too hot.
The whistle blows
its warning:
such very ugly houses.
But in that corner
of the window,
the ice-white,
eternal promise
of a new moon.

Fauré's Second Piano Quartet

On a day like this the rain comes
down in fat and random drops among
the ailanthus leaves—"the tree
of Heaven"—the leaves that on moon-
lit nights shimmer black and blade-
shaped at this third-floor window.
And there are bunches of small green
knobs, buds, crowded together. The
rapid music fills in the spaces of
the leaves. And the piano comes in,
like an extra heartbeat, dangerous
and lovely. Slower now, less like
the leaves, more like the rain which
almost isn't rain, more like thawed-
out hail. All this beauty in the
mess of this small apartment on
West 20th in Chelsea, New York.
Slowly the notes pour out, slowly,
more slowly still, fat rain falls.

INDEX OF FIRST LINES

INDEX OF TITLES

THE NEW YORK POETS